PUTTING *U*P WITH

MR. RIGHT

PUTTING *U*P WITH

MR. RIGHT

LEN McMILLAN ✦ MARVIN WRAY

How to Build
Love, Friendship, and Intimacy

REVIEW AND HERALD® PUBLISHING ASSOCIATION
HAGERSTOWN, MD 21740

The author assumes full responsibility for the accuracy of all facts and quotations as cited in this book.

Unless otherwise credited, all scriptural passages are from the *Holy Bible, New International Version*. Copyright © 1973, 1978, 1984, International Bible Society. Used by permission of Zondervan Bible Publishers.

Bible texts credited to RSV are from the Revised Standard Version of the Bible, copyright © 1946, 1952, 1971, by the Division of Christian Education of the National Council of the Churches of Christ in the U.S.A. Used by permission.

Bible passages credited to Clear Word are from *The Clear Word* paraphrase of the Bible by Jack Blanco, copyright © 1994 by Jack J. Blanco.

This book was
Edited by Richard W. Coffen
Designed by Bill Kirstein
Cover photo by D. Degnan/H. Armstrong Roberts
Typeset: 11/13 Times

PRINTED IN U.S.A.

00 99 98 97 96   5 4 3 2 1

R&H Cataloging Service
McMillan, Leonard David, 1938–
   Putting up with Mr. Right: how to build
love, friendship, and intimacy, by Len
McMillan and Marvin Wray.

   1. Husbands. 2. Marriage. I. Wray,
Marvin, joint author. II. Title.

      306.872

ISBN 0-8280-0967-8

Contents

CHAPTER 1

Can This Be My Man?

Have you ever wondered how your Mr. Right friend can sometimes seemingly read your mind, yet be so dense a few moments later? It can be frustrating trying to relate to the
opposite sex. One woman recalls a particularly challenging situation.
"My husband and I hadn't had a date for at least two months. Our mutual birthday time had arrived, and I had planned a surprise party for
him with a small group of friends who were to meet us at a familiar
Chinese restaurant. With the baby-sitter armed with instructions and
snacks, we headed for the car. Behind the wheel my husband suggested, 'Let's go for Mexican food!' That would have been a delightful idea, except that our friends would be waiting at the other
restaurant. I tried to remain unruffled and replied sweetly, 'I think
Chinese sounds better tonight.'

"'No,' he replied swiftly, 'I want a big enchilada!'

"After some haggling, it became apparent that he'd chosen tonight
to be demanding, un-
reasonable, and inter-
ested only in his own
food cravings. Dark
thunderclouds formed
inside the car. Finally I
screamed in frustra-
tion, 'You dope! I
have a surprise party
planned at the Chinese
restaurant. We have to go there.'

> *Growing persuasive
> evidence indicates that some
> aspects of our personality are
> more genetically based than
> learned.*

"He laughed—and that made me even angrier. He laughed so hard
it took him five minutes to tell me that he'd planned a surprise party for
me, too—at the Mexican restaurant. It was the one fact I didn't know.
Now whenever I'm tempted to be impatient with him, or anyone else

for that matter, I try to observe the 'one fact' rule: Look for a hidden fact that might offer a logical explanation for obnoxious behavior."

Actually, you probably know your man well enough to predict with almost uncanny accuracy how he will react before you speak or make your request. This chapter will help you understand more fully why Mr. Right's actions (or reactions) may border on the absurd at times.

• • •

Each of us is a product of both heredity and environment. However, growing persuasive evidence indicates that some aspects of our personality are more genetically based than learned. The old adage "Like father, like son" has more than a degree of truth to it. Studies of twins have been popular during the past two decades and have dramatically influ-

> *The evidence indicates that someone who is bitter and grouchy at 20 is, without active efforts to change, likely to be bitter and grouchy at 80, despite having every apparent sign of success.*

enced the study of temperaments. The most informative studies involved identical twins who were separated at birth and had never met again until they were brought together by researchers. These studies found that identical twins raised apart could be more alike than fraternal twins raised together!

Evidently we are all given a unique DNA identification tag at conception that identifies us throughout our life. We can certainly modify our behavior and change objectionable traits, but a common thread seems to run through our life, which researchers can now trace from birth to the grave.

You might think (and hope) that people would become more open-minded, more agreeable, and less neurotic as they mature. Unfortunately the evidence indicates that someone who is bitter and grouchy at 20 is, without active efforts to change, likely to be bitter and grouchy at 80, despite having every apparent sign of success. Likewise, people with sunny dispositions tend to stay cheerful all their lives, in spite of setbacks and tragedies.

The main ingredients of temperament tend to remain stable throughout a lifetime. What you see in your man today is likely to be what you'll see in him 20 years from now. However, many women view the potential—rather than reality—in their man when selecting a companion. Unfortunately for both of them, she may spend the rest of her life trying to change him into what he *ought* to be. Such wishful thinking is like trying to teach a pig to sing—it only makes you frustrated and the pig angry!

While it is true that many male traits are learned from family or culture, it is also true that some traits of character remain constant throughout a lifetime. Aggressive men have often learned as boys that aggressiveness will bring them what they want—attention, toys, dominance. And they have learned how to be aggressive by imitating their parents or television actors. Grown-up boys, from Donald Trump to John McEnroe, have learned these lessons well. In a less competitive and aggressive society their temper tantrums would not be tolerated, but in our society they are often held up as the epitome of manhood.

Our attempts to discover how much behavior is inherited versus how much is learned won't be fully successful in the near future. The purpose of this chapter is not to make that determination, but to alert you that some inherited temperament traits will probably remain constant and resistant to change. It is a waste of time and energy to try to reprogram anyone's biological inheritance tag, including your own. Likewise, the excuse "I can't help it; that's just the way I am" is also invalid, since behavior can be modified. The bottom line is: We can do a great deal about changing our own behavior, but very little about changing someone else's behavior.

If you're in a relationship with a man, and you think he might make a good life companion after you smooth out some of his character flaws, start looking for another man. It is both presumptuous and foolish to enter any relationship with the purpose of changing the other individual. Most psychologists today agree that small changes and improvements in personality—tune-ups of the mental transmission—are possible, but total transformation is not.

You can help facilitate many changes, such as better communication skills, recovery from trauma, constant irritability, or even low self-esteem. But you must learn to live with more basic traits or find yourself a more compatible companion. The greatest lesson genetics can teach us is to appreciate the diversity of human beings and to accept built-in limitations. This chapter will assist you in your struggle to know what is changeable and what is inevitable in Mr. Right's temperament traits.

> *We can do a great deal about changing our own behavior, but very little about changing someone else's behavior.*

• • •

As you begin this study it is important to know that no man (or woman, for that matter) is a single temperament type. We are all blends. However, one or two temperament types will usually predominate in his lifestyle and decision-making. The following temperament types are arranged from the most outgoing (Sammy Seller) to the most reserved (Robert Relater). They will give you insights into both learned and inherited tendencies.

Sammy Seller (Strengths)

Sammy Seller is an energetic, talkative storyteller who lives for the moment. He is keenly focused on the present and is usually the life of the party. Seller exudes charisma from every pore of his body. Everyone seems to be attracted to him. He has a childlike optimism, always seeing the best in everyone and everything. Seller appears to be relatively innocent and easily persuaded. He thoroughly enjoys life and seldom recalls the hurts or disappointments of the past.

Sammy Seller is a constant toucher. In fact, he finds it extremely difficult to keep his hands off other people. Superfriendly and sincere, he makes his way through life while good-naturedly bouncing off from every obstacle in his way. He makes an excellent actor because he's always on stage. Seller is likely to be envied by those around him, since he apparently enjoys every minute of life. Those brief moments that are not enjoyable (such as breaking up during dating) are soon forgotten in the thrill of a new moment or conquest.

Aggressive and future-oriented, *Donald Doer* is likely to be a workaholic in his areas of interest. He is constantly in motion and never seems to tire. A courageous crusader, Donald will often try to rectify every perceived injustice that is in his area of interest.

Endowed with tremendous enthusiasm and charm, Sammy Seller inspires others. In fact, no one will start more projects than Sammy. Unfortunately, he seldom finishes any of them. The charming Seller makes friends easily and probably was voted the most popular guy in high school. However, you should remember this word of caution: *No one can love you more or forget you faster than Sammy Seller.* He thrives on compliments, does not hold grudges, and sincerely loves practically everyone. If for some reason he should lose his temper,

Sammy Seller *is an energetic, talkative storyteller who lives for the moment. He is keenly focused on the present and is usually the life of the party.*

he'll probably apologize profusely a few minutes later and then take you out to lunch or bring you flowers.

Donald Doer (Strengths)

You will immediately recognize the strong willpower of *Donald Doer*. Aggressive and future-oriented, he is likely to be a workaholic in his areas of interest. If it is sports, he will strive to be the best. If it is scholastic achievement, his GPA will reflect his dogged determination regardless of his IQ. If it is a career, that will become the focal point of his life. Donald Doer is constantly in motion and never seems to tire. In addition to being self-sufficient and independent, he has a compulsive need to change his environment, along with an urgency to correct all the wrongs in the world. A courageous crusader, Donald will often try to rectify every perceived injustice that is in his area of interest. A born leader, he is also an excellent judge of people. This is unlike Sammy Seller, who views everyone (including you) through rose-colored glasses. Born with the flame of eternal optimism, fanned by his supreme self-confidence, Donald Doer doesn't know the meaning of the word "defeat." Whether in a career or marriage, Donald must succeed. If he meets with any failure, it cannot be his fault. He will always find a scapegoat upon whom to place the blame.

Unemotional and goal-oriented, Donald Doer lets nothing stand between him and success. If you happen to get in his way, look out! A great organizer and delegator of work, he is often put in charge of projects that would send a lesser person into spasms of insecurity. Donald thrives on competition and even opposition. Oppose him, and you'll reap the whirlwind. Doer knows only one way to play any game (including the game of life), and that is to win. Excelling in emergencies, the unemotional Donald Doer usually makes the right choices and often leads his family, team, or corporation into the winner's circle.

Unfortunately, hard-driving Doer seldom has time or need for close friends. Even though he may have many acquaintances and even admirers, he generally uses people as tools to accomplish his numerous goals. Those on his list of friends will often feel both compelled and privileged to help Donald accomplish a worthy task.

Tommy Thinker (Strengths)

The sensitive and talented *Tommy Thinker* can be very emotional and is usually in touch with the moods and needs of others. He may be a latent genius just waiting to be discovered. Serious and purposeful in life, Tommy experiences both the heights of ecstasy and the pits of despair. Conscientious and idealistic, he strives for perfection in everything. Tommy Thinker will be a loyal, lifelong friend, and if you're on his list of friends, you're one of the select few. During his entire lifetime he seldom makes more than a handful who qualify as true friends.

Tommy Thinker is often referred to as a detail hound because of his penchant for minute perfection. Tommy's complete attention to detail often drives fun-loving Seller into temporary exasperation. Thinker usually feels the need to make certain every *i* in life is duly dotted.

Tommy Thinker is always on time. He follows a schedule and is seldom late to work or any appointment.

> **Serious and purposeful in life, Tommy Thinker experiences both the heights of ecstasy and the pits of despair. Conscientious and idealistic, he strives for perfection in everything. Tommy will be a loyal, lifelong friend.**

He is orderly, organized, and uncommonly neat. Other descriptive words include "consistent" and "dependable." While often very creative, Thinker must wait for the artistic mood to strike before accomplishing his finest work. You'll quickly notice that he finds it difficult to engage in recreation if he has unfinished work waiting elsewhere. Thinker does not like to be hurried into doing anything less than a perfect job. In fact, anything less than absolute perfection may be considered a complete failure.

Content to stay in the background, Tommy Thinker makes a good support partner for Doer or Seller, neither of whom can tolerate detail work. Tommy will listen sympathetically to complaints, exhibiting sincere concern for friends and, on occasion, even complete strangers. His sensitive nature and ability to discern is especially important in the temperament mix of any family or business, since Donald Doer often leaves a lot of walking wounded in his wake as he powers through the waters of life on his way to the island of success.

Robert Relater (Strengths)

The easygoing, witty *Robert Relater* can see humor in the most mundane situations. Born with a superb sense of timing, Relater can keep you in stitches without his ever cracking a smile. His low-key personality wears well, and he is usually welcome in a group. Cool, calm, and collected, Relater is both dependable and consistent. He usually keeps his emotions hidden and appears to be happily reconciled to life. Robert is supportive as a friend and is often considered the ideal son or husband.

> **The easygoing, witty Robert Relater *can see humor in the most mundane situations. His low-key personality wears well, and he is usually welcome in a group. Cool, calm, and collected, Relater is both dependable and consistent.***

Perhaps no one is more dependable during a crisis than Robert Relater. Seldom one to become upset over uncontrollable circumstances, he exercises great patience and calmness when others are going out of their mind. Robert is a natural problem solver and mediator who works well under pressure. These traits give him natural administrative ability, but he seldom is chosen for that position early in his career. Most organizations seem to promote first flashy Seller or determined Doer. However, after serving in an organization for a few years, Relater often finds that his natural temperament traits propel him into administrative or supervisory positions. Always efficient and neat in his chosen areas of interest (the rest of his lifestyle may resemble the aftermath of a hurricane), Relater is highly valued as a friend and confidant.

Thus far we have summarized the basic strengths of the four temperament types. Unfortunately, since sin entered our gene pool in the Garden of Eden, temperament has another side, often referred to as weaknesses but usually more accurately defined as sinful tendencies.

Sammy Seller (Weaknesses)

Being a compulsive talker, *Sammy Seller* is often described as entering a room "mouthfirst." In fact, he not only tends to bore others with trivia, but often cannot recall names and constantly exaggerates when telling his favorite stories. In fact, the more often he tells the story, the more unlike the truth it becomes. His happy-go-lucky attitude may cause others to distrust him, because he seems phony and untrustworthy. His loud voice and blustery complaints can be an embarrassment at times. Superegotistical, obnoxious Seller loves to talk about himself. Emotionally unstable, Sammy cries almost as easily as he laughs. In fact, he may switch from intense anger to a contrite plea for forgiveness so rapidly that he appears to be out of control, or at least insincere, to Doer and Thinker.

As one who would rather talk than work, Sammy is also weak-willed and undisciplined. His lifelong motto is "If it feels good, do it!" Although his mind is usually filled with hundreds of ideas, he's often a disaster when it comes to implementing those ideas. He tends to forget obligations, appointments, assignments, and resolutions because of the distractions of the moment. Unfortunately, Sammy Seller seldom lives up to his potential or your expectations.

> *Being a compulsive talker, Sammy Seller is often described as entering a room "mouthfirst." His happy-go-lucky attitude may cause others to distrust him, because he seems phony and untrustworthy.*

Unable to determine his own limitations, Seller often bites off more than he can chew. When asked to volunteer, his initial response is yes! However, his lack of organizational skills, combined with his time-wasting habits, makes Sammy a candidate for failure unless he learns self-control. Lack of self-control is the basic success ingredient missing in his life. Because he is so easily distracted, he often finds it difficult to set or maintain priorities. He always intends to do the right thing, but he never seems to get around to it. Sammy may be the most intelligent guy in school or the smartest man in his corporation, but if he doesn't acquire self-discipline, he will always be a success waiting to happen.

Seller needs both a stage and an audience. He hates to be alone and fully expects everyone he meets to like him. After all, he likes himself, so how can anyone else (with any taste at all) not like him? He wants to get credit (even if it isn't due him) and may become sullen if slighted. Sammy tends to dominate a conversation, fails to listen (since he is too busy preparing his next eloquent monologue), answers questions before they're asked, gives answers for others, interrupts constantly, and repeats his stories ad nauseam. Add to this list fickleness and forgetfulness, as well as the tendency to make excuses for his failures, and you have an all-too-accurate picture of Sammy Seller's weaknesses or sinful tendencies.

Donald Doer (Weaknesses)

Donald Doer has the well-earned reputation for being bossy, arrogant, impatient, quick-tempered, and explosive, and for carrying a grudge. It has been said that Doer will have an ulcer before he's 40 and will have given ulcers to 40 others (including his spouse) by that time. He often launches projects that he later regrets, but his pride will not let him admit a mistake and start over. Because of

Donald Doer *has the well-earned reputation for being bossy, arrogant, impatient, quick-tempered, and explosive, and for carrying a grudge.*

his tenacity to hang in there even after he should have let go, he'll often succeed, but sometimes at a terrible cost to himself and others.

Donald enjoys controversy and arguments. Since he doesn't know how to lose gracefully (or any other way, for that matter), he plays to win. This usually limits his friends to those who can overlook his competitive nature or who receive some benefit from the friendship. Doer despises those who cry or show their emotions, even though he often displays the emotion of anger. Lacking any real sensitivity, he views expressed emotions as a sign of weakness in others. Self-sufficient, haughty, and proud, Donald can be extremely obnoxious and quite unsympathetic.

Often in charge of a small business, the entrepreneur Doer has little tolerance for mistakes by others. Since he never makes mistakes himself, it never occurs to him that someone else should be allowed to use failure as a learning experience. Bored by trivia, he avoids reading instructions and often makes hasty decisions based on insufficient data. Once made, however, these decisions are cast in concrete and will be defended until death. While often rude and tactless, Donald can be very charming when it's to his advantage. His charm is usually evident during dating or courtship, when he is trying to attain a goal, but it often fades quickly once the goal has been achieved. Unlike Seller, who tends to use things to influence people, Doer uses people to accomplish things. In addition, Donald Doer expects and often demands complete loyalty and obedience.

He also has an irritating tendency to make decisions for others, often without their consent. Since he usually assumes that he has superior knowledge in the matter (even if he doesn't), he'll feel justified in making a decision for you and others. Donald Doer also tends to be very possessive of anything he might consider his personal property. That may include you or even his friends. Since he seems unable to pronounce the s word (sorry), it is very difficult for him to apologize. He reasons, "Why should I apologize when I'm not wrong?" Sadly, he may exhibit the same reluctance to show approval or give compliments. These characteristics may make Donald unpopular and even feared by those who know him well.

Tommy Thinker (Weaknesses)

Tommy Thinker finds it extremely difficult to forget the past and to plan for the future. He is extremely sensitive and often feels offended, even when no offense was intended. Tommy also has a very difficult time dealing with anger or frustration.

I (Len) have often compared Thinker to a cow chewing her cud. One of the more memorable recollections from my childhood involved watching my father's cows eat. I soon learned that when a cow chews her cud, it means she's actually eating her food for the second or third time. Since a cow has a number of stomachs that contain food in various stages of digestion, she burps up the food she has already eaten, chews on it awhile, and then swallows the masticated mass to store it in another stomach. A cow does this repeatedly until all her food is fully digested.

Tommy Thinker follows the same procedure when dealing with anger or frustration. Rather than confront the source of his anger

Tommy Thinker *finds it extremely difficult to forget the past and plan for the future. He is extremely sensitive and often feels offended, even when no offense was intended.*

directly, he swallows hard and walks away. But later, in private, he "burps" up the incident, recalls it in living color, and lets his anger run wild. This procedure may continue almost indefinitely unless his anger is finally resolved. Eventually some unlucky person (perhaps even you) will come into Tommy's presence just after he has "burped," and this hapless individual will receive the full fury of undigested wrath.

It may sound strange, but Thinker actually seems to enjoy playing the martyr. Perhaps because he often has a low self-image, he may feel more comfortable in the martyr's role and even view it as his inevitable and just reward in life. While this role may make him appear humble to others, Tommy may actually possess a false sense of humility based upon his proud perfectionism. In other words, since Thinker cannot live up to his own expectations (unfortunately, neither can anyone else), he may appear humble to others when he points a derisive finger at himself. However, his pursuit of perfection will also make him very demanding as a work supervisor or spouse.

Tommy Thinker often suffers guilt, *guilt*, GUILT! He may even have a persecution complex. He tends to develop a rather pessimistic attitude toward life. His constant self-examination may turn him into a hypochondriac, finding illness and symptoms where none really exist.

Whether at home, school, or work, Thinker prefers to work alone. He often seeks out a little corner to himself, rather than being in the middle of a busy room. Once he finds such a secluded spot, he can accomplish much. Not afraid to tackle difficult assignments, Tommy is a definite plus for any organization as long as he isn't in constant contact with other people. He prefers analysis rather than busywork. He needs to know that what he is doing is important and really makes a difference. However, unlike Donald Doer or Sammy Seller, he does not desire the spotlight. Tommy Thinker would rather be an appreciated support person producing high-quality work. Even though he may be difficult to please, his high standards enable him to produce superior work. Tommy must constantly be reassured that he's truly appreciated. A solid compliment each day will motivate him to even greater levels of productivity both at work or in a relationship.

In social circles Thinker may appear somewhat withdrawn and even remote. He tends to live his life vicariously through others. Tommy usually dates and eventually marries Sally Seller or Doris Doer. Born with a suspicious nature, Thinker often holds back affection and inwardly resents opposition. Even though he desires and needs compliments, he is often skeptical and may impute ulterior motives when a compliment is given.

Robert Relater (Weaknesses)

Robert Relater openly displays very few weaknesses because of his charming personality and easygoing lifestyle. Unlike the more visible Doer or Seller, he's more reserved, and one must look deeper and longer to determine the effects of sin in his temperament. Relater often lacks motivation, enthusiasm, and decision-making skills. He does not like to get involved, and may also avoid responsibility; and he can be as stubborn as a Missouri mule. While often viewed as shy and retiring, no one can be more set in his ways or more self-righteous. Although some see him as compromising, Robert is actually a peace-loving individual who dislikes confrontations of any sort.

Because he lacks motivation, Relater may depend on others to point out his tasks or work assignments. While this works quite well in the predictable structure of a classroom, it may become a problem later in life as he enters the workplace. Some refer to Relater as the original energy conservationist. No one can conserve energy better than Relater, especially if it's his own! He actually resents being pushed into any work assignment that was not his idea or that he is reluctant to perform. Viewed as somewhat careless and lazy, his laid-back attitude may be a source of irritation or even discouragement for a spouse or friend.

While Robert tends to be somewhat unexciting as a friend or life partner, his dry sense of humor keeps him in high demand. However, his tendency to tease and judge in jest can sometimes strain a relationship. Usually attracted to Sally Seller or Doris Doer, he may frustrate his more progressive companion with his built-in tendency to resist change or to accept new ideas and concepts.

Robert Relater *often lacks motivation, enthusiasm, and decision-making skills. He does not like to get involved, and may also avoid responsibility; and he can be as stubborn as a Missouri mule. While often viewed as shy and retiring, no one can be more set in his ways or more self-righteous.*

In this brief overview of the four temperaments you have probably found your male friend, spouse, and a few good friends. Maybe you've gained some insights into yourself at the same time. It is important to state again that no one is a single temperament type. Therefore, when discussing temperaments or analyzing your Mr. Right, don't expect him or others to fit neatly into one classification or another. This knowledge of inherited tendencies will be useful as you attempt to understand yourself, your man, and others.

• • •

Some studies have reported research on various body types that might prove helpful in trying to understand your man. While much in this field of study is anecdotal or speculative, the following information may prove entertaining even if it does lack scientific agreement or support.

Sammy Seller often possesses what is called the "G" type body. His chest predominates, since the heart and lungs need air and space (remember, Seller enters a room mouthfirst). He tends to like spicy, creamy foods that stimulate his sex glands. His favorite facial expression tends to be lively, and he's a great improviser.

Donald Doer's body is often dominated by bones and muscle. A born leader, his type "A" body is often stocky or full-figured. He is a high-energy person who tends to stimulate the adrenal gland with salty food or red meat. (If vegetarian, I suppose he eats kidney beans!) His facial expressions tend to be severe, even though, like Seller, he is active and easily excited.

Tommy Thinker may have a body dominated by his head and nervous system. Known as the "T" type body, he tends to have full hips and thighs, with slender arms and legs. To activate the thyroid gland, he prefers sweets and starches. His sensitive nature may lead to a nervous condition or even depression at times. His facial expressions are often anxious or stressful.

Robert Relater's body is often dominated by his digestive system. (Isn't that a pleasant thought?) Even though he usually eats rather slowly, his digestive system is often troubled. His "P" type body may have baby fat and small feet. He tends to eat dairy products to stimulate the pituitary gland. His generally passive nature is mirrored through his calm and serene facial expressions.

Although body type may not specifically identify your man's behavior, it can provide some entertaining discussion that may reveal further insight into his temperament blend. As you observe his facial expressions, use these "windows" to help you understand his underlying agenda and temperament traits. You might want to use body types as a discussion tool when he's in a good mood—just for fun!

• • •

Unfortunately, as sinful human beings we all share a common problem that must not be overlooked in our quest for understanding: "Our natural tendencies, unless corrected by the Holy Spirit of God, have in them the seeds of moral death" (Ellen G. White, *The Ministry of Healing,* p. 455).

Jesus reminded Nicodemus (and us): "Truly, truly, I say to you, unless one is born anew, he cannot see the kingdom of God" (John 3:3, RSV). It is important for us to realize that even though we were born with the seeds of moral death already within us, God has provided a solid solution to our dilemma. "There is therefore now no condemnation for those who are in Christ Jesus" (Rom. 8:1, RSV). Isn't that *good news?* It might even make your day. I know it makes mine every time I read that promise. However, this good news does not excuse bad behavior. It was meant to change behavior!

"A noble, all-around character is not inherited. It does not come to us by accident. A noble character is earned by individual effort through the merits and grace of Christ. God gives the talents, the powers of the mind; we form the character. . . . Conflict after conflict must be waged against hereditary tendencies. . . . A character formed according to the divine likeness is the only treasure that we can take from this world to the next" (Ellen G. White, *Christ's Object Lessons,* pp. 331, 332).

> *It is important for us to realize that even though we were born with the seeds of moral death already within us, God has provided a solid solution to our dilemma.*

Transformation of character does not change temperament blend, but it does transform the temperament we were given at birth. "Man

CAN THIS BE MY MAN?

23

is not endowed with new faculties, but the faculties he has are sanctified." "A new standard of character is set up—the life of Christ." "The natural inclinations are softened and subdued. New thoughts, new feelings, new motives, are implanted" (Ellen G. White, in *Review and Herald,* July 7, 1904).

The good news is that Jesus came to amplify our God-given strengths and to eliminate our sinful tendencies. Remember Paul's desperate cry for help: "Wretched man that I am! Who will deliver me from this body of death?" (Rom. 7:24, RSV).

> *Jesus came to amplify our God-given strengths and to eliminate our sinful tendencies.*

His answer provides insight into the whole process of transformation: "Thanks be to God through Jesus Christ our Lord! . . . There is therefore now no condemnation for those who are in Christ Jesus" (Rom. 7:25-8:1, RSV).

As you review your own temperament blend and that of your Mr. Right, with all their strengths and weaknesses, remember that Jesus came to make both of you into a new creation. During this restoration process He does not eliminate the identifying characteristics of your unique temperament blend. Instead He preserves everything about your temperament blend that is inherently good and seeks to eliminate those areas influenced by sin.

When we are born again, our temperament will surely be altered, but *we will not change temperaments.* God has a particular temperament blend in mind for you and another for your man. It is not the temperament blend that causes problems; it is sin, which has attached itself to our genes like a parasite. This parasite of unwanted tendencies is transmitted from generation to generation. The good news is that God promises to remove that parasite from both you and your man so completely that it's even removed from your record in heaven (1 John 1:9).

Once we are born again, the need to use a persona (false mask) slowly diminishes as Jesus begins the restoration work in our life. It becomes less and less necessary to cover up our real selves. The character change that begins inside of us eventually manifests itself in our outward actions. Therefore, as we grow in Christ, we have fewer sinful parasites to hide and more of the inner beauty God originally intended for us becoming evident. We may not notice the change, because we're too close to the battle, but others will notice.

Remember that no one is a single temperament. None of us fit neatly into a single temperament type. We are all unique blends. "We differ so widely in disposition, habits, education, that our ways of looking at things vary. We judge differently. Our understanding of truth, our ideas in regard to the conduct of life, are not in all respects the same. There are no two whose experience is alike in every particular. The trials of one are not the trials of another. The duties that one finds light, are to another most difficult and perplexing" (Ellen G. White, *Gospel Workers,* p. 473).

> *As we grow in Christ, we have fewer sinful parasites to hide and more of the inner beauty God originally intended for us becoming evident.*

According to the laws of genetics, the chances of two people being exactly alike are about one in 300 billion. So even though we can identify general characteristics and similarities in each temperament type, no one, including your man, fits neatly into that package. However, a general knowledge about temperament types should help you better understand your own actions as well as those of everyone around you.

Paraphrasing Florence Littauer, we can remember temperament strengths this way: Thinkers *invent* a product, which is *manufactured* by Doers and later *sold* by Sellers to be *enjoyed* by Relaters. Temperament weaknesses may be summarized in this manner: Sellers *enjoy* people and forget them; Thinkers are *annoyed* by people but let them go their own way; Doers *use* people to accomplish their goals and afterward ignore them; Relaters *study* people with haughty indifference.

A knowledge of temperament types should make you more understanding and tolerant of your friends, your family, your man, and yourself. As God's Spirit continually fills your life, you will become even more aware of that cancerous malignancy of sin dwelling within. But the good news is that Jesus is working right now to remove that malignancy and make you whole again. Claim this precious promise whenever you sense that sin has taken over your body: "If we confess our sins, he is faithful and just, and will forgive our sins and cleanse us from all unrighteousness" (1 John 1:9, RSV).

Another promise worthy of memorization and daily recall is: "For whatever is born of God overcomes the world [sinful tendencies]; and this is the victory that overcomes the world [sinful tendencies], our faith. Who is it that overcomes the world [sinful tendencies], but he who believes that Jesus is the Son of God?" (1 John 5:4, 5, RSV).

Claim these promises daily with Mr. Right and ask God to help you both be all that He intends for you to be in Christ Jesus!

CHAPTER 2

Head Hog
at the Trough!

H ello," answered the church secretary. "How may I help you?"
"I want to speak to the head hog at the trough!" boomed a
male voice.

"You want to what?"

"I want to speak to the head hog at the trough!"

"Do you mean our pastor?" asked the stunned secretary.

"Yep! I guess I do."

"If you want to speak to our pastor, you'll have to show a little
more respect," responded the secretary emphatically.

"I'm sorry," the male voice replied more softly. "I just wanted to
give him a $10,000 donation for your church building fund."

"Please don't hang up. I think I see the big pig coming now!"

What does it mean to be head hog at the trough? First among
equals. Numero uno. Head of the class. The decision-maker. The
mover and shaker. Power broker. Whatever term one uses, the pecking order isn't determined by drawing names out of a hat. In the family unit it depends upon two major factors: genetic inheritance and
birth order.

A recent study indicates that genetics shape our personality three
to five times more than does home environment. In fact, Dr. Robert
Plomin, of Pennsylvania State University, states that the home training accounts for less than 10 percent of our total behavior patterns.
Plomin and his colleagues tracked a sample of 99 identical twins and
229 fraternal twins who were reared apart. They matched this sample
against 160 identical twins and 212 fraternal twins who were raised
together in the same home. The average age of both samples was 59,
and it is the largest study of its kind. Here are some of the findings
(from *U.S.A. Today,* Jan. 11, 1989).

1. Those raised in *restrictive* homes tended to have their personalities molded more by the parent(s) and less by genetics. As ex-

pected, those raised in *permissive* homes were the most likely to reveal inherited tendencies and qualities.

2. Even though children grow up in the same home, they do *not* experience the same environment.

This study seems to confirm that domineering parents shape the personality (and lives) of their children more than do permissive parents. It also revealed that children from restrictive/domineering families are more likely to have problems with social skills and acceptance.

One factor not studied by Plomin was the birth order of the twins as they related to other siblings in their natural or adopted families. Dr. Kevin Leman has written an informative book on this subject. He divides siblings into three categories: firstborn, middle child, and lastborn (see *The Birth Order Book*).

> **Domineering parents shape the personality (and lives) of their children more than do permissive parents.**

Researchers have tried to establish a strong relationship between birth order and specific occupations, for example, but they just have not found one. However, many more subtle net effects of birth order can be more easily understood as the "pecking order" of a community.

Family rules and roles continue to regulate behavior long after individuals have become adults. People seem to carry their family of origin rules into their adult relationships and even into the workplace. Likewise, the birth order roles that people occupy in their families of origin can influence their functioning, relational patterns, and the kinds of family systems that they form in their adult lives. Birth order roles are learned in the family and tend to be assumed in situations outside the family. Recent research indicates that by understanding roles and patterns in families of origin, family members can better understand themselves as individuals and how they relate at work or play or worship.

Hägar the Horrible, the comic strip Viking, is talking to his men, trying to pump up their courage before the ensuing battle. "This will be a dangerous mission, but anyone who refuses to go will be forever branded a cowardly, weak, gutless, soft, fainthearted, cringing, trembling wimp!"

Hägar's little buddy, Lucky Eddy, replies, "I can live with that."

While the exact amount that home influence exerts upon behavior patterns is open for debate, most would agree that it does play an important role in establishing values and social skills. It may even be an important factor in creating dysfunctional behavior patterns at a very early age. Therefore, understanding the family pecking order of your Mr. Right can be a helpful tool to help you understand his values, social skills (or lack of them), pet peeves, quirks, and even obnoxious behavior.

> *A typical firstborn is a perfectionistic, conscientious, list-making, well-organized, goal-oriented, self-sacrificing, and reliable leader.*

Larry Leader (Firstborn)

A typical firstborn is a perfectionistic, conscientious, list-making, well-organized, goal-oriented, self-sacrificing, and reliable leader. New parents expect a great deal from their first child, as well as from themselves. Everything was the *first time* and became terribly important. The baby shower, nursery wallpaper, purchase of clothes, selection of a name, and even establishment of a college fund were all important events for these first-time parents. Encyclopedia salespersons found them easy prey and may have even sold them a set that would be outdated before the firstborn learned to read. Even the grandparents may have gotten caught up in this momentous occasion and tended to overdo for the firstborn. Consequently, this new branch on the family tree became the leader and standard bearer for the rest of the family.

To conclude that Mom and Dad expected more from their first child is logical, but to conclude that certain behaviors are inherent in a firstborn overstates the case. The family pecking order is important in establishing behavior patterns and values, but it isn't composed of inherited characteristics. Birth order is important because it helps us understand how family units relate to each other, but inherited temperament traits are far more important for determining and understanding the whole individual. As family units become smaller and the number of one-child families increases, the importance of birth order will tend to diminish.

Research indicates that firstborns actually walk and talk earlier than their other siblings. Is it any wonder, with every adult in the family ecstatic over their every "goo-goo"? Perhaps firstborns learn to walk earlier in order to put distance between themselves and the constant adult prodding. Since firstborns have only adults as role models, it seems logical that they'd pick up adult behavior. With no other siblings to challenge their authority, firstborns assume that control is their God-given right.

Larry Leader, 3 years old, is standing on a chair in the kitchen, taking a brownie from the counter. At that moment Mom walks through the door and sees her guilty son with has hand in the cookie

Birth order is important because it helps us understand how family units relate to each other, but inherited temperament traits are far more important for determining and understanding the whole individual.

jar. "Those brownies are for dessert. I don't want to see you taking any," she utters matter-of-factly.

Larry thinks for a minute and replies, "Can't you just turn your head?"

Firstborns develop confidence (even arrogance) at an early age. Their confidence level is increased at an early age when they may be called upon to be baby-sitter or even surrogate parent for their younger siblings. It is almost as if firstborns never had an opportunity to be a child. Perhaps that explains why 52 percent of all presidents of the United States and an even larger percentage of corporate executives are firstborns. They are natural leaders, and their early responsibilities as the oldest sibling enhanced their leadership ability.

Firstborns tend to have an edge in the overachiever department. Bill Cosby, a true perfectionistic firstborn, named all his children with the letter *e* to remind them to pursue excellence in life. Phil Donahue calls himself "controlling"; he also is a firstborn. A survey of 92 local talk-show hosts revealed that 87 were firstborns. Martin Luther King, Jr., was certainly driven and displayed many firstborn characteristics.

However, not all firstborns exhibit the same degree of leadership. Other factors, such as inherited temperament blend, parental discipline style, culture, and peer group all play a role in determining behavior. Leman suggests that there are at least two types of firstborns: *compliant* and *strong-willed*.

Compliant firstborns are often viewed as model children. Besides being conscientious and reliable, they utter such reassuring phrases as *Yes, Dad! Yes, Mom!* and *Thank you!* Compliant firstborns have a strong need for approval and usually become good students or workers.

My (Len's) wife, Karen, is a compliant firstborn. Actually she's an only child, which certainly makes her a firstborn. I'm a strong-willed firstborn. Our temperaments and behavior patterns are opposite, yet we both display firstborn tendencies. When we eat at a restaurant and the food is cold or poorly prepared, I'll ask for a replacement. This embarrasses my wife, who would rather eat cold food than create a scene.

Strong-willed firstborns need to be the center of attraction even before leaving their mother's womb. They are classic type A personalities and begin to make their desires known with frequent kicks and turns before they are born. Later they may become workaholics, addicted to the adrenaline of a hard-driving personality. Even personal ads become obvious when written by firstborns.

"Christian, blond, blue eyes, 5'2", 100 lbs. prof., cauc./female, no dependents, wishes to meet Protestant Christian, prof. man in 30s with college degree who has compassion for animals and people, loves nature, exercise, and phy. fitness (no team sports), music and dance, church and home life. Desires nonsmoker/nondrinker, slender, 5'7"-6', lots of head hair, no chest hair, intelligent, honest and trustworthy, sense of humor, excellent communicator of feelings, very sensitive, gentle, affectionate, androgynous attitude about roles, giving, encouraging, and helpful to others, no temper or ego problems, secure within and financially, health-conscious, neat and clean, extremely considerate and dependable. I believe in old-fashioned morals and values. If you do too and are interested in a possible Christian commitment, write to P.O. Box 82533. Please include recent color photo and address."

Isn't it interesting how perfectionism can narrow one's vision? Perhaps the writer of that ad would have been

The majority of people in counseling are frustrated first-borns burdened down with guilt.

more successful by reading the latest edition of Grimm's *Fairy Tales*.

A friend of mine once made a fortune establishing a company from virtually nothing. He operated out of his home for years and eventually sold the business for several million dollars. Yet even after becoming a millionaire, he seldom took time to enjoy his financial success. Workaholics are goal-oriented and thrive on the next challenge. However, their addiction to making decisions and always being right makes it very difficult for them to accept rejection or criticism. Apparently these traits, pushed to their extreme, eventually prompted the biblical firstborn, Cain, to murder his younger brother. Jesus reminds us that murder comes in many forms and can be performed with the tongue as well as with a knife. Many firstborns practice murder with their tongue and may prove difficult to live with.

Leman states that the majority of people in counseling are frustrated firstborns burdened down with guilt. In their attempts to be perfect for their parents, perfect for their siblings, perfect for their teachers, and now perfect for their spouse, typical firstborns may expect or even demand perfection in the relationship.

If you're in a relationship with—or married to—a strong-willed firstborn, you may need to establish some personal territorial boundaries. Unless you establish certain boundaries in your relationship, you may risk becoming a doormat rather than a partner.

Many firstborns have never learned to say "I'm sorry!" These words do not come easily to proud, in-charge firstborns. Helping Mr. Right master that phrase may prove difficult. Like the Fonz from the old TV sitcom *Happy Days,* he may have difficulty expressing the s word—sorry. It may be even more difficult for him to ask, "Will you please forgive me?" Often firstborns, at an early age, develop a view of God as a stern enforcer of laws who is unable to accept anyone who isn't perfect. While this unfortunate portrayal of God's character is inaccurate, it may greatly influence a firstborn's relationships, including his relationship with you.

Norman Negotiator (Middle Child)

Lucy set up her psychiatric advice booth, where she offered advice for a nickel.

Charlie Brown inquired, "Lucy, I need help."

"What can I do for you, Charlie Brown?"

"I'm confused. I can't seem to find a direction, a purpose for life."

"Oh, don't worry, Charlie Brown. It's like being on a big ocean liner making its way through the sea. Some folks position their deck chairs to face the front of the ship, and others place their chairs to face the side of the ship or the back of the ship. Which way do you face, Charlie Brown?"

Charlie responds sadly, "I can't even unfold the deck chair."

Middle children are born into a dilemma. Just about the time they get used to being the youngest child, someone else takes over that coveted position in the family. Middle children are born too late to get all the privileges and special attention offered to firstborns and too soon to enjoy the relaxed discipline afforded to lastborns.

Middle children often exhibit what psychologists refer to as the *branching-off* effect. If the older sibling is more intelligent in a certain area, middle children will branch off in a different direction. If middle children are one of many children, they'll look at the directions already pursued by their older siblings and more often than not choose a different route. While all siblings play off the firstborn, they also must be concerned about all others who are older in the family. This can have a dramatic effect on the portrayal of their natural temperament blend. If their temperament blend conflicts with a role already taken in the family pecking order, they may choose to suppress their natural inclinations in order to be different.

It may be said that middle children get no respect. They're the Rodney Dangerfields of siblings. A typical family photo album has three times as many pictures of the firstborn or lastborn as it does of the middle child. One 13-year-old middle child had just fallen into puppy love with the boy next door. She went to the family album to find a picture and eventually yelled in frustration at her mother, "Aren't there any pictures of me without her?"

> *Middle children are born too late to get all the privileges and special attention offered to firstborns and too soon to enjoy the relaxed discipline afforded to lastborns.*

Friends often become the extended family of middle children because they don't hold the coveted first or last position among siblings. To obtain reward and recognition, middle children turn to friends. (Firstborns typically have fewer friends, because parents and grandparents have supplied that need.) Middle children often engage in team sports or join a gang to find recognition and a sense of belonging. They often leave home at an early age to avoid the frustration of being average.

Because middle children learn to negotiate and compromise at an early age, they often grow up to be well-adjusted adults. However, their penchant for peace may actually condition them toward codependency. Even though middle children may need professional help as adults, they will seldom seek it unless coerced by someone they care deeply about. While firstborns demand help and lastborns expect to be cared for, middle children develop a spirit of independence and mental toughness that doesn't allow them to accept assistance, except occasionally from friends.

Middle children are great negotiators; they learn at an early age how to make relationships work. This often influences them to take seriously both monogamy and commitment.

Even though being a middle child is a relatively safe position, it is often unfair. Therefore, middle children tend to view life through reality lenses rather than fantasy glasses. Unlike firstborns and lastborns, who often have a distorted view of life, middle children expect little from life and therefore are seldom disappointed. Because firstborns have run interference for them, middle children often relate to a more relaxed parent. Balance is a key element throughout the life of middle children.

If you are in a relationship with a middle child, it's important to refrain from the comparison trap. Comparing your man to other men is futile and pointless at best, while absolutely devastating and destructive at its worst. Your man probably has already developed good listening and negotiating skills because of his position in the family. Promote and develop those skills in your relationship. Since negotiators and compromisers often make the best managers or leaders, encourage your middle child man to make the most of his abilities in these areas.

> **Because middle children learn to negotiate and compromise at an early age, they often grow up to be well-adjusted adults. However, their penchant for peace may actually condition them toward codependency.**

Charlie Charmer (Lastborn)

A small lastborn child, assigned to the attic bedroom, was frightened during the night by a loud thunderstorm. After being assured by his mother that God would take care of him, the little boy replied, "Well, you come up here and stay with God. I want to go down and sleep with Daddy."

It's difficult to argue with outgoing, charming, manipulative, affectionate lastborns. They are usually the family clown or attention-getter, and, according to the other siblings, spoiled rotten. The family curse on lastborns is to be forever viewed as both the smallest and the weakest. Often you will see a five-foot-six-inch firstborn introduce a six-foot-five-inch lastborn as "my little brother"! This perspective often prompts lastborns to go through life constantly looking for praise and encouragement. Like Mark Twain, lastborns can often live a month off a good compliment.

> *It's difficult to argue with outgoing, charming, manipulative, affectionate lastborns.*
> *They are usually the family clown or attention-getter, and, according to the other siblings, spoiled rotten.*

Of all the sibling positions, lastborns are the most likely to be people-oriented. Studies indicate that the babies of the family tend to gravitate toward people-oriented jobs. Leman tells about a used-car salesman who was so bubbly and friendly that he often sold the most cars each month without even trying. However, the manager (a firstborn) was constantly haranguing him about getting in his paperwork. Finally a psychologist suggested to the manager that he hire a secretary to do the paperwork for his top (a lastborn) salesman and let him do what he did best, relate to people. A survey of the used-car lot revealed that all the salespersons were lastborns trying to work for a workaholic firstborn, who was making their lives miserable by his constant demand for paperwork.

If you have a relationship with a lastborn, are you demanding or insisting that all the "paperwork" be done before he can enjoy people?

The independent cockiness displayed by lastborns is often an attempt to cover up their inner confusion. Impetuous and brash, lastborns rush in where angels fear to tread. They seldom consider the consequences before taking action. Their reaction in times of trouble may provide evidence of their people skills, especially in the area of manipulation.

A teenage lastborn was arriving home well after curfew. As he neared the house he shut off the car lights and coasted quietly to a stop. Creeping into the house, he removed his shoes and slipped quietly down the hall. It was 2:00 a.m., and just before he got to his room, a light came on and his mother called out, "John, what time is it?"

"It's midnight, Mama," he replied. But just at that moment the cuckoo clock let out two cuckoos. Without the slightest hesitation, John stood in the hall and cuckooed 10 more times!

As the friend of a lastborn, you can help him accept responsibility for his actions. Allowing Charlie Charmer to reap the consequences of his immature or childish actions is often a persuasive instructor. Perhaps you find it easier to perform a task (which he considers unpleasant) yourself rather than allowing it to remain undone. Actually, you're doing him a great disservice when you perform this function for him. Lastborns will romp merrily and irresponsibly through life as long as conscientious firstborns are around to perform the unpleasant tasks.

Allowing Charlie Charmer to reap the consequences of his immature or childish actions is often a persuasive instructor.

A little lastborn was smarting after being punished by his father for being obnoxious in front of house guests. Shortly afterward the father tucked him into bed and knelt with him as he said his prayers. The prayer ended with the usual blessings for all the family members except one. Then the mischievous lastborn turned to his father and announced, "I suppose you noticed that you weren't in it!"

Learn to appreciate Charlie Charmer's timing and sense of humor. Everyone else will.

The question many women ask at this point is If I am contemplating entering into a relationship with a man, what birth order would be the best for me? Actually, it probably plays a rather insignificant role when compared to inherited characteristics, which you might find much more difficult to adapt to or change than "pecking order" behavior. However, Leman suggests in his book *Were You Born for Each Other?* that a firstborn will usually do well marrying a lastborn, and middle borns will probably do well regardless of birth order because of their ability to compromise and negotiate. Once middle borns are married, according to Leman, they tend to stay married.

> *If you wish to know how your man will talk to you after marriage, listen while he talks to his younger sisters or brothers.*

In any event, it's important to examine Mr. Right's "family tree" as well as the "pecking order" if you truly want to understand him. When relatives say "He acts just like his uncle Charles," find out what they mean by that statement. As you discover how his family relates to each other, you will learn a great deal about his ability (or lack of ability) to communicate in a manner you find acceptable. If you wish to know how your man will talk to you after marriage, listen while he talks to his younger sisters or brothers.

Many firstborns, for example, are torn between loving and honoring their parents and disliking them at the same time. They often cannot forget that their parents were much harder on them than on their younger siblings. Although the middle child will usually be a negotiator, he may also be suspicious of a compliment and wonder what you really want. The lastborn may be so wrapped up in being the center of attention that you'll get very little of the spotlight. A careful look at your man's family will enhance your understanding of him.

It's important to remember that your man is unique, no matter what his birth order or temperament blend. You are both a combination of many factors: inherited temperament characteristics, birth order, culture, friends, and parental style, to name a few. Interestingly enough, when studying our similarities we often also discover our uniqueness.

Perhaps your man can identify with a chubby middle child competing at a school track meet. The participants were in the final lap of a boys' one-mile run. The pack was bunched together except for two runners, who were leading by a few yards. As they rounded the last corner, the crowd was cheering wildly. Amid all this excitement it was easy to overlook a short, chubby kid running hopelessly last. He probably had difficulty walking a mile, much less running one. Nevertheless, there he was, pushing toward the finish line as his contorted, red face revealed the supreme effort he was putting forth. It appeared that his face and entire body might actually explode at any moment.

As you attempt to understand your man, it's important that you show appreciation for the best effort he can put forth.

Suddenly a frantic woman pressed through the noisy crowd, jumped up on the railing, and screamed, "Johnny, run faster! Run faster!" Her shrill voice carried audibly above the din of the noisy crowd. Obviously she was the poor boy's mother.

Upon hearing his mother shrieking at him, a hopelessness came across Johnny's face. You could read the silent reply in his countenance. *Run faster? Run faster? If I could run any faster, do you think I'd be dead last? Just what do you think is my problem, Mom? Do you think I just forgot how to run? I'm running as fast as I can!*

As you attempt to understand your man, it's important that you show appreciation for the best effort he can put forth. It isn't important for him to act like your father, your brothers, your friends, or anyone else. He's one of a kind!

• • •

Stereotypes are always dangerous, particularly when one uses them to assess manhood. Every man is different and must be accepted as such. The man who responsibly toils day after day at a job he detests in order to support his family may not feature a charismatic constitution or physical "animalism," but he may be more of a man than the body-builder or television actor who may abandon his family responsibilities to satisfy his own selfish desires.

It's always wrong to assess only one area of a person's life, and it's even worse to compare one individual to another. Since God gave your man his uniqueness, you will both be happier if you first concentrate on discovering who he is, accept him as he is, and finally trust God to modify any areas that He (not you) deems in need of improvement.

According to sociologists, everyone resists change. That is particularly true if someone else is arbitrarily trying to force some change upon us. Any temperament or manhood modifications must come from within your man as prompted by the Holy Spirit, rather than by endless criticism from a fellow sinner.

Psychologist Carl Rogers offers a useful analogy: "When I walk on the beach to watch the sunset, I do not call out, 'A little more orange over to the right, please,' or 'Would you mind giving us less purple in the back?' No, I enjoy the always-different sunsets as they are. We do well to do the same with people we love" (cited in Alan Loy McGinnis, *The Romance Factor*).

CHAPTER 3

I Work, Therefore I Am!

In case you haven't guessed it by now, something is going on among the men in America. Change is in the offing. Not subtle, insignificant change, but giant, rumbling change. Men have formed a movement. The movement is relatively new, but I (Marvin) believe that the desire for it is longstanding. Many, perhaps even most, men have wanted to be more in tune with the needs and feelings of their families. They want to be sensitive, but nobody has taught them how to do it in a masculine way.

Dr. Jan Halper, a management consultant in San Francisco and author of *Quiet Desperation: The Truth About Successful Men,* has interviewed more than 4,000 male executives, managers, entrepreneurs, and other professionals. She has found that "men have gotten a lot of bad press over the past few years. They're seen as insensitive, uncaring, out of touch with their feelings. These men are questioning the choices they've made in their lives. They are changing, slowly and silently. They want to reach out for more, . . . but they don't know how" *(Privileged Information,* Mar. 1, 1990, p. 7).

She further states that 60 percent of the high achievers she had interviewed said that if they had it all to do over again, they wouldn't live the same way. So obviously we are not talking about every man. We are never talking about every man. But we are talking about a significant number who have put in enough years to achieve some measure of success, and they are looking around and asking, "Who am I? Where am I? What have I done? Where is my family?"

Some who have given all to the work ethic have been turned aside and replaced by younger men or by technology. Others have been mergered out. Many who are still around feel empty inside. What's the problem? Their identity has been in their work. They are what they do.

I work, therefore I am.

How old was I? Three? Four? Five? I don't really remember how old I was when people started asking me, "What are you going to be when you grow up?" They meant well when they asked, and I've asked the question of boys too and added thereby to the perpetuation of the burden. I wish I had known to say, "I'm going to be a man." They undoubtedly would have clarified, "No, son, I mean what are you going to do?" Because for most men "to be" means "to do."

First, I was going to be Superman. I can remember tormenting my older sister by tying a dishtowel around my neck, "flying" over the coffee table, and landing on the couch, where she was trying to color. She sure didn't respond like Lois Lane! If she could have gotten her hands on some Kryptonite, she would have made me eat it.

As I matured I was going to be a cowboy, a policeman, a fireman, and then a mechanic, like my dad. He was unimpressed with my first three choices and adamantly opposed to the last. He wanted me to be "better" than that. "Go to school. Study hard. Get an education and make something of yourself." He wanted me to do better—that is, make more money than he did.

Two things in particular were, and still are, very important to my dad, and he drummed them into me: a work ethic and staunch masculinity. He wanted me to achieve in school so that I could work with my head rather than my hands, because that would probably mean a better wage scale, but the bottom line was that I work hard. I must be dependable and reliable. Added to that, I must act like a man. No "sissy stuff" allowed. From the age of about 5 it was no more kiss good night. We shook hands. I don't ever remember calling him anything but his first name, Rolly. That's still what I call him.

By the time I was 7 I had decided that I wanted to be an engineer who would design and build great buildings or bridges. That was met with widespread approval. It was OK *to be* an engineer. Anyone who now knows my home improvement skills will get a real chuckle out of that, but the point wasn't whether or not I had the skills. The point was the identity.

All through junior high and high school I excelled at math, and that was good. The problem is that I have the mechanical aptitude of a dyslexic chimpanzee. (My apologies to the chimp.) So finally I went off to college to become a teacher. That was OK. Not great, but permissible. Our relationship was going through some strain at that time anyway. I dropped out of college my senior year because I was terrified at the prospect of becoming something that I really didn't want to be. I drove a truck, sold pianos and organs, sold life insurance, sold men's suits, even sold Fuller Brush supplies. Finally, after I met and married Ingrid, I landed a management training position with Bank of America in California. Dad was really happy with that!

I still tend to measure myself by what I do and how well I can do it.

Less than a year later I called my parents and told them I was leaving Bank of America to go back to college. "Great! You going to study math?"

"No, Dad."

"Well, you going to become a teacher?"

"No, Dad."

"Well, what, then?"

"I'm going to study for the ministry."

It was not a particularly affirming conversation from that point on. My dad wasn't exactly what you would call a man of the church, and to have to explain to his friends that he had sired a pastor was not a pleasant prospect.

Nearly a quarter century has passed since then, and he still introduces me as his half-wit preacher kid. But he does say it with pride. He won't admit it, but he does.

Don't misunderstand me. I am not blaming my father in any way for any struggles I may have had or still may have with my identity as a man. He taught me what had been taught to him and what was important from his perspective. I don't fault him for that in any way. In fact, it shows that he did care.

The fact remains that I still tend to measure myself by what I do and how well I can do it. What am I going to be when I grow up? I don't know. When I get there, I'll let you know.

• • •

In my heart I believe I am a man. I'm God's man. I'm a husband, a father, a grandfather, a brother, a son, an uncle, and a friend of many. I'm a lover, a runner, and a collector of books. I teach, I preach, I listen, and I care more deeply about you than I can often express. My soul cries out just *to be* and not be at all measured by what I do.

At a spiritual retreat for pastors 54 of us gathered for five days of just being together, looking at ourselves, and worshiping God. We came from a wide variety of denominations and ministries, and the beautiful thing was that not once did anyone ask anything about our work. We shared names, families, hurts, needs, time, and space. I didn't want to leave.

There's something freeing about being anonymous. In AA and other similar support groups people may come and share common needs without identifying anything about themselves. They don't even have to talk about their problem. It is assumed, understood, and accepted. Maybe men need an "Identity Anonymous" group to join. They could come together on a first-name basis only. No one would ask what they did. They'd just acknowledge by being there that they were sometimes frustrated, sometimes weak, sometimes erring, sometimes hurting men. Everyone would understand and identify.

Ladies, did you know you can do some powerful things that will have a positive impact on each of the men in your life?

Ladies, this is a really heavy and complex area of men's lives. Your dad is, or was, affected by *doing* to *be*. Likewise your son is or will be, and so are all the other men in your life. Did you know you can do some powerful things that will have a positive impact on each of them?

Start by peeling off the labels. How often do you hear—or use—phrases like these? "This is my son, the doctor." "This is my father, Professor Know-It-All." "Have you met my brother, the model?" It does help tie in the identity, but often the tie is used to make a point. You're proud that your son is a doctor. Nobody blames you for that. He has worked hard to achieve that, and probably so have you. If you have another son who picks up people's trash, do you introduce him as "my son, the garbage collector"? That's why we have new titles like sanitation engineer. We don't have cooks; we have culinary artists.

Most work identities have stereotypes too. Treasurers are tightwads. Car salespersons are shysters. Doctors are snobbish, and truck drivers are rough. Kids even get caught up in it. Mine grew up as PKs, or preacher's kids. It's not a label they're particularly fond of. Do you like to be known only as Ray's wife, Bob's daughter, Jimmy's mom, or Ted's sister? How often has my wife been introduced simply as the pastor's wife? I wish I had a dollar for each time. She refuses to be offended, but will step

> **Make a deliberate conscious decision to separate Mr. Right from what he does. Tell him again and again that you love him no matter what.**

forward and say, "Hi, my name is Ingrid. What's yours?" Make a deliberate conscious decision to separate Mr. Right from what he does. Tell him again and again that you love him no matter what.

I have grown exceedingly weary of bumper stickers informing me that the driver has an honor roll student at Lahteedah Elementary School. I saw one recently that said, "My son beat up your honor roll student." I'm not supporting the action, but I did have to affirm the humor displayed by a fellow nauseated traveler. How would I react to a sticker like "My son is the vice president of IBM"? Who cares?

Men are tired of playing the "What do you do?" game. We said "I do" at the altar. Let us be secure in that and in all the other relationships that union has brought about rather than in our current ré-sumé of "I do's." We still play the game because we don't know how to get out of it. We obviously need to be speaking to the men themselves as well, but you need to be part of the change.

Don't get caught up in it yourself. Women are starting to be pretty good at the "What do you do?" game these days too. Some wives are intimidated by it and will answer, "Oh, I'm just a house-wife." Others, seeking affirmation of their position, refer to themselves as domestic administrators.

Another positive action would be to encourage all the men in your life to participate with other men in community groups and organizations in which what one does is not nearly as important as what one is doing. Dads who are at or near retirement age will especially benefit from such relationships as their job identity begins to fade away.

One leader of men's seminars purposely instructs the men to keep their occupations secret during their time together. This brings home the point rather quickly as to how much they define themselves by title. They find they have a great deal in common with other men from widely varied backgrounds.

In one such seminar two men who'd been fierce competitors and had built up strong resentment toward each other, although they had never met, found themselves at the same table, unaware of anything other than the first name of their partner. When the seminar ended and last names were revealed, both were in for quite a shock. They admitted that they had hated each other for years without knowing each other and now were faced with the dilemma of having developed a friendship.

Mothers, suggest that your sons practice concealing their dad's occupation with people they meet. Make a game of it. When friends ask them, "What does your dad do?" have them give answers like "He mows the yard and helps mom with the dishes sometimes." Or "He plays catch with me."

When you meet other men and they identify their occupation, try asking them such questions about their work as "Do you like your work?" "What do you like about your job?" "If you could start over and do anything you wanted, what would you do?" Strive to get to the person behind the mask.

Do you perceive the men in your life as successful? My dad was a very successful mechanic. Now he's retired. Is he still successful? Yes! He is enjoying his restructured life. That answers it for me. Men do want to be successful in the work that they do. Obviously, if they can't do the work successfully, they really ought to try something else. But you can affirm men as successful people, no matter what level of achievement they have in other areas.

> *If your idea of success is centered in being first or in ranking high, there will by very few, if any, successful men in your life.*

Every year more than 10,000 people line up on Hayden Row in Hopkinton, Massachusetts, with a goal to run 26.2 miles through Ashland, Framingham, and Natick. They'll run through the gauntlet of women at Wellesley College near the halfway point. (I've seen runners backtrack so that they could do this twice!) They'll pass through Newton and struggle up "Heartbreak Hill." At Boston College they level out again and head down Beacon Street. A few more miles, a few more turns, and finally they're on Boylston, and the roar is deafening. They cross the finish line, and each runner receives a medal. Which one is successful? Is it the winner? Perhaps it is each age-group winner.

I'm sure you'll agree that each finisher is successful. We all recognize that many who took five or six hours to finish worked harder and showed more raw courage than the fleet sub-five-minute-mile paced winners. But what about the 1,000-plus runners who don't make it to the finish? Are they successful? Yes! Because they got out of their easy chairs and tried.

If your idea of success is centered in being first or in ranking high, there will be very few, if any, successful men in your life. It is good to encourage your men to have high goals, but show them that their identity, their success, is in whether they participate in the race of life and whether or not they enjoy the people lining the course.

To me, it's the hundreds of thousands of people who make the Boston Marathon great. It's the kids holding out orange slices and ice cubes and hands eagerly wanting to slap a high five. It's the folks spraying hoses and the volunteers handing out sponges and cups of drink. It's the bands and the jugglers and the clowns taking your mind off the pain. It's the police officer at the top of Heartbreak Hill who says, "It's all downhill from here." (It isn't.) It's the man pushing his adult palsied son in a wheelchair the whole distance so that he too can take part in life. It's Jack Kelly, who is running it for the fifty-eighth consecutive year. It's people, and that's life.

Help your Mr. Right concentrate on his participation in life rather than on some imagined finish line. Men seem to be programmed to *conquer* a task. On vacations we tend to have a destination goal and will ignore all but the most urgent cries to stop. ("Billy is starting to throw up!" will usually do it.) We often take much the same approach to life itself, as if it were only a task to be completed. Help your men prioritize their goals. Make sure that the goals you have set for them are balanced as well. Not only will the world continue without my putting in a 60-hour week, but most of us can probably survive very

Those who have faced a life-threatening health problem likewise tend to have taken a serious look at what's really important.

well with fewer things and with a less-than-perfect house. Keeping things in balance is always a good goal in life.

Interestingly, Dr. Halper found that the men who were the most satisfied and content with their lives were those who had survived at least one personal trauma, such as being laid off, fired, divorced, or had lost a child or spouse to death. Those who have faced a life-threatening health problem likewise tend to have taken a serious look at what's really important.

How easily we all get caught up in our goals and overlook the joy of living! This is true of men from all age groups, and as the workplace and opportunities keep changing, we see it happening to women as well. Equal opportunity means equal pitfalls, also.

A friend of mine who is a Christian career counselor likes to have clients play the "And then what?" game. He begins by asking, "What do you want to do next?"

When they are able to identify a particular step, he asks, "And then what?"

They will continue to outline goals that eventually will lead them to "Well, I guess then I'll retire."

"OK, and then what?" he counters.

This gets them thinking about their own personal dreams and enjoyments. But he still doesn't stop. Eventually they're left with nothing but "And then I die."

"And then what?"

Boom! Yeah, and then what? What's it all about, anyway? Where are we going, and what are the stops along the way?

You might want to try the "And then what?" game with some of your favorite men. It's a good conversation starter. It's not a bad idea to play it yourself.

Since I am addressing a wide variety of women, let me give you a few ideas to apply to your own lives and to influence further the lives of men you care about.

Help your Mr. Right verbalize his dreams. Focus on one or two and see if you can help him make them a reality. Support him in taking a risk, and be there for him if he should fail.

Seize the moment—It's always good to dream and set goals, and it's always good to reflect and evaluate. But consider stopping to celebrate some of life's events as they happen. Life is pretty short at best. Have a party once in a while to acknowledge some achievement or some good thing that might be easily overlooked in the mad dash for the pot of gold at the rainbow's end.

A news reporter said that Bill Clinton's response, when nominated by the Democratic Party for president, was "God doesn't give you many days like this!" I'd say that's a pretty good attitude. It would be easy to get caught up in the vision of the next goal and the scramble to achieve it. Better to take the time to celebrate today.

Risk it—Life is short! Don't be afraid to take a chance occasionally. No one wants to put things of value in jeopardy, but I talk to a lot of people who look back and wish they had given some dreams a chance instead of always walking in the safe, familiar rut.

Help your Mr. Right verbalize his dreams. Focus on one or two and see if you can help him make them a reality. Support him in taking a risk, and be there for him if he should fall. Perhaps there's no greater failure in life than never to have tried. Do you have a young man or a widowed father who is attracted to a member of the opposite sex? Give him a nudge. Let him know that she'd be the lucky one. How about a husband or brother who's stuck in a meaningless job? Help him look at all the options, even the far-out ones. Don't let your Mr. Right become marooned on Someday Isle—"someday I'll try this;" "someday I'll change that." The truth is, someday he'll look back and wonder what else he could have done, and there will be no tomorrow.

Let God make a difference—If we really do seek God's kingdom and His righteousness first, it should make a difference in how we approach life. Worldly ambition should become less dominating as lives are committed to His control. Let Him take the heavy burdens and provide the rest He promises. The quality of our work will increase, but the motivating factor will be our desire to lead a life that honors God rather than to elevate ourselves or to accumulate things.

Charles Spurgeon, pastor during an earlier generation, usually chaired a membership committee in his church that interviewed prospective members. One woman who worked as a maid was asked the question "How do you know that you have repented of all your sins?"

She quickly replied, "Because now I don't sweep the dirt under the carpet."

That's spiritual ethics! Our connection with Christ *does* change the way we approach our work. It also gives us new identity. We're no longer men of the world involved in *being* by *doing*. "Now we are children of God, and what we will be has not yet been made known. But we know that when he appears, we shall be like him" (1 John 3:2).

Isn't that a great promise? Work is a task assigned by God even before the entrance of sin in the Garden of Eden, but it was never meant to be our identity. Affirm your man in his struggle to let go of earthly pressures and to set his sights a little higher.

> *You can help him see that his identity is much more than his work. Help your man realize that your love and value for him are unconditional.*

Build self-esteem—One of the great tragedies of modern times is that too many of us find little real enjoyment and pleasure in what we do. Some surveys report that as many as 90 percent of men see themselves as caught in a trap from which they cannot escape. They are victims of a society rather than contributors to it. If a man's identity is in his work and he hates what he does, how must he feel about himself?

You can help him see that his identity is much more than his work. Help your man realize that your love and value for him are unconditional. If he's a Christian, remind him that God's presence with him makes any work a calling, rather than merely a job. It's rather like the man mixing cement on a large construction project who was approached by the general contractor. The man in charge asked the workman, "What are you doing?"

Not knowing to whom he was talking, the man mixing cement said, "Can't you see? I'm building a great cathedral."

Help your man see his role in God's overall plan. No matter what his task or assignment here on earth, if he dedicates himself to God it is not menial or degrading. Jesus chose laborers and government employees to be His closest associates. He doesn't ask "What do you do?" He asks "Will you walk with Me?"

What about the ladder?—Every man has a mental picture of a ladder that he must climb, and he knows which rung he's on. He's also acutely aware of the position of those around him. He often sees his family, particularly the women, as holders of the ladder. Their job is to support him while he climbs. The problem is that the higher he climbs, the more distant he becomes. Husbands want wives to balance their ladders, and wives want husbands to balance their priorities. It's a precarious situation. There are two times the ladder is most significant.

The first is when a man is young and is beginning his ascent. He is excited and full of dreams, energy, and desire. He has something to prove. He is on his way up. Whether he is in the business world or the workplace, he has his eye on accumulating everything he can— money, points, contacts, and things. You need to affirm him and support the concept that this is the time for him to show that he can do the work and that he does have a future. You also need to help him provide for his future at home.

A young couple can endeavor to make home a place in which they'll both want to be. The key is in talking it through together. Not just before you are married and during the first few months, but again and again. Talk and evaluate. Reflect and talk.

A mother or aunt or simply an older friend can help a young man by encouraging him to pace himself well. Offer the opportunity for him to see what went well and what didn't in your own life. Encourage him to seek the friendship and mentorship of men who have already been down the road. As a friend of mine put it, help him find the companionship of a man "who has finished well."

The second dangerous moment on the ladder is when a man realizes either that he is not going to make it as high as he had dreamed or that the top is an illusion. In his book *Passages*, Gail Sheehy tells of a middle-aged newscaster who had achieved national recognition but had found that the snow on the top of the mountain he had conquered was, in reality, not snow at all but salt.

This is the time of burnout, midlife crisis, and difficult decisions. Some men will press on in a futile effort to climb higher. Others will just put in their time, but they go dead inside. Some will be tempted to jump and end it all, and still others will try to recapture their youth and begin all over again with new challenges—and too often with a new woman.

At this time Mr. Right may need all his women working together in his life. The wife, mother, daughter, sister, and friends will need to encircle him with love, understanding, affirmation, and a real

Happiness is not often found on the next rung of the ladder if you don't already possess it.

sense of being needed. Help him see what he has achieved. Perhaps he *has* reached the top of his particular ladder. Help him explore his options. There may be new areas of work to explore and new risks to take, but help him do it in the counsel of others who care about him. Also, take the time to sit with him and count your blessings. Happiness is not often found on the next rung of the ladder if you don't already possess it.

One of my very favorite stories illustrates the point well, though I take some risk in repeating it here.

A little bird was not well and was unable to make the trip south with the larger group. When he finally recovered, he decided to try it on his own. The weather had turned cold; and flying alone, without the protection and encouragement of the flock, he soon was too exhausted and weak to continue, and so he landed in a barnyard. He realized that he was not going to make it and reconciled himself to his dismal fate.

About that time one of the barnyard cows walked by and buried the poor discouraged creature in a very undignified substance. Our fine feathered friend was really bemoaning this unpleasant occurrence when suddenly he realized that he was no longer cold. In fact, he felt quite warm! He also discovered little particles of food unused by the previous owner, which he—ever so carefully, mind you—picked out to eat until he was not only warm but also full.

Now, this was such a positive turn of events that he began to consider that he really was a fine fellow after all. He began to be proud of how he had handled the situation, so he lifted his voice in song to show that he was indeed a survivor. Just at that moment the barnyard cat happened by, heard the singing, cleared away the pile, found our little traveler, and promptly ate him. Sad indeed!

There are three morals to this story. First, not everyone who dumps on you is your enemy. Second, not everyone who cleans you up is your friend. Finally, if you have the good fortune to be warm and full, it's best to keep your mouth shut.

Help your man discover that happiness is found neither in flying with the flock nor in toughing it out on his own. Real happiness is found in recognizing the wonderful provisions that God makes for each of us. If we feel like singing, let it be in praise to God for His love, mercy, and grace.

CHAPTER 4

Hi, Mom!

From the beginning of time more male babies than female have been born. This would seem to give men a decided edge in the population department. Wrong! By the age of 18 the numbers of men and women are about equal, and from that point on women have a decided majority because of their longevity.

Since sin entered the world it appears that men have also enjoyed more power in the male-female relationship. Wrong again! Men only *thought* they were in charge of their destiny as well as that of their family, community, and nation.

During the fifties and sixties women made hot breakfasts and packed nourishing lunches for their husbands. They laundered the clothes, shopped for groceries, cleaned the house, and cooked the meals. Women developed a reputation as taxi drivers for their children. Afternoons were spent washing, waxing, and ironing—or volunteering at the local hospital. Women concentrated on becoming "good" housewives and pleasing their husbands.

Men came home from a hard day at the office or factory, plopped down in their favorite chair, and were waited on by their wives. They read the paper, spent a few minutes with the kids, and watched a little television as their wives prepared the evening meal. After supper the men might wash the car or mow the lawn, but little else. Later the family would gather around their black-and-white television set to watch *Ozzie and Harriet, Leave It to Beaver,* or *Father Knows Best.* Many even believed that father really did know best.

Women served, supported, and sustained the home. Men reigned, regulated, and ruled over everything from the factory assembly line to the household allowance. Men made money; women spent it. In all matters of major expenditures, men made the final decisions. Men kept the bank accounts, took out insurance policies, and filed the income tax.

Women who worked outside the home did so as schoolteachers, nurses, clerks, secretaries, and librarians. They took orders from men who were principals, doctors, managers, or owners. Women received little or no medical benefits or retirement plans. Even Social Security was male-dominated. The family was taken care of by the male head of household. Women, even though employed, focused mainly on their families and the home. A very limited number of single women actually seemed to pursue a career.

Marriage was permanent, but fidelity was not, at least for the man. A wandering male was winked at, but his female counterpart was viewed as a slut or worse. Even rapes were often blamed on the female, who, it was claimed, acted or dressed in a seductive manner.

Men are still dependent upon women to define their manhood. During the past 50 years, only women have changed in any significant manner!

A cursory examination would seem to indicate that men had it pretty good in those days.

Today this scenario seems somewhat absurd. Nearly every detail of the family structure has changed dramatically, except one. Men are still *dependent* upon women to define their manhood. During the past 50 years, only women have changed in any significant manner! Many men, contrary to the evidence so easily attainable, still assume they're in control. Men often bluster about with grunts and other indescribable sounds in order to give the illusion of being in control. But that's all it is, an illusion!

The only man in human history who was *not* dependent upon a woman was Adam. Since the creation of woman, man has been totally dependent upon woman for his existence. From the womb to the grave, man needs woman much more than woman needs man. Man is conceived inside woman, develops securely in her womb, nurses at her breasts, and is instructed at her feet. On Mother's Day five times more cards are sent and telephone calls dialed than on Father's Day. Even male athletes who have just made a game-saving play often dedicate that play to their mother by shouting into the camera, *Hi, Mom!*

Men are infatuated by, dependent upon, and often obsessed about women. The average teenage male thinks of sex 20 times an hour. Men spend much of their life searching for the

> **A man spends the first half of his life trying to separate from his mother and the last half trying to understand that separation.**

intimacy that they feel only a woman can provide. In male-female relationships today, the vast majority of men find themselves stuck between a rock and a soft place. Women are successfully redefining their understanding of womanhood, while men are still attempting to maintain an illusion of power and control. As one man commented: "All men are frauds. The only difference between them is that some admit it. I myself deny it."

When forced, a man may reluctantly make some minor revisions to the myth of manhood, but the emphasis is usually on the word "minor." Men sometimes voice support for the changes going on in women's lives. Many actually *believe* they are activists in bringing about change, but how men really *feel* is often a different story.

A man says: "I don't expect my wife to do everything around the house as my mother did." But he's feeling: *I'm tired at night, and I want somebody to give me love and support when I get home.*

A man says: "Of course we should have an equal relationship." But he's feeling: *As long as I am first among equals.*

A man says: "I'm proud of my wife for earning more money than I did last year." But he's feeling: *What would the guys think if they knew? Besides, she really doesn't need me anymore.*

When a man states emphatically, "It's not the money; it's the principle," it *is* the money; or "I'm not mad, but . . . ," he *is* mad;

or "I don't depend on women," he *does* depend on women.

It would be helpful for women to understand that men are not intentionally deceptive in this matter. Cliché and common wisdom seem to tell us that it's a man's world. The accepted mythology of many males is that men are independent, women are dependent; men are dominant, and women submissive; men make history, and women provide emotional support. Real men don't depend on women. Real men stand alone!

Men continue to believe this myth because they fail to acknowledge the primal power women wield over them. The average man spends a lifetime denying, defending against, trying to control, and reacting to the power of a woman.

The secret men seldom tell—and often don't know on a conscious level—is the extent to which their lives revolve around their relationships with women. A man spends the first half of his life trying to separate from his mother and the last half trying to understand that separation.

Woman is the center around which a man's life revolves. She's the audience before whom man plays out his life. She's the judge who pronounces him guilty or innocent. "She is the Garden of Eden from which we are exiled and the paradise for which our bodies long. She is the goddess who can grant us salvation and the frigid mother who denies us.

Men are more disturbed by the woman in their heads than the woman in their beds or boardrooms.

She has a mythic power over us. She is at once terrifying and fascinating" (Sam Keen, *Fire in the Belly,* p. 15).

Men have invested an extraordinary amount of time and energy trying to control, conquer, avoid, or demean women in a relentless attempt to make themselves less vulnerable to women's seemingly mystic powers over them. Men emerged from women, and they fear that they may once again merge with them. In a futile attempt to prove themselves invulnerable, they often build up walls of resistance and deny their God-given emotions and feelings. One author equated women as black holes into which the male psyche is inevitably drawn until it disappears altogether.

Men are more disturbed by the woman in their heads than the woman in their beds or boardrooms. The real problems in male-female relationships are created by myths and misinformation about each other. Denial of a woman's power over man only increases her power over him.

Woman was, is, and always will be the source from which man comes. All human beings come from the warmth of her womb. The earliest images of woman portray her as a divine being—a mother-goddess that makes men feel impotent. Compared to women, men have relatively little to do with the procreation of the human race. Men often envy and sometimes view with awe women's capacity to give birth. Humankind has even endowed the earth with female qualities and refers to its mysteries as Mother Nature, not Father Nature.

Much of the meaning men attribute to their work may be a futile attempt to match women's ability to give life. Instead of life, men's fruitless search leads to competition, wars, and male posturing.

Men often accuse women of penis envy, but the male is often subjected to womb awe or even womb worship. While most men seldom spend a conscious moment wishing they were female, they are still overwhelmed by the ability of women to conceive, carry, and deliver a baby. Birth gives meaning to her body in a way that sowing seed does not give meaning to his body. She makes a significant contribution to the presence of life, while he must content himself with lurking on the periphery.

A young father-to-be was pacing back and forth, wringing his hands in the hospital corridor, while his wife was in labor. He was tied up in knots of fear and anxiety, and beads of perspiration dropping from his worried brow revealed the agony of his suffering. Finally, at 4:00 a.m. a nurse popped out of a door and exclaimed, "Well, sir, you have a little girl!"

The man dropped his hands, became limp, and replied, "Oh, how I thank God it's a girl. She'll never have to go through the awful agony I've had tonight."

Women smile knowingly at this story. Men feel the punch line in their gut. The only thing a man brings to the birthday party is his own impotence and inability to make a significant contribution to this great event.

Unable to create life, men create machines. Much of the meaning men attribute to their work may be a futile attempt to match women's ability to give life. Instead of life, men's fruitless search leads to competition, wars, and male posturing.

Humankind is born recognizing the mother as the one who gave life to them. A newborn male (or female) infant is programmed for immediate face recognition and will spend most waking moments focused on mother. Her face becomes the infant's radar to the world. Her expression will reveal what is good or what is bad. Her eyes will express joy or sorrow. Her anger will judge and her smile reward the baby. A severe, disapproving glance will strike terror in the heart of almost any child.

A mother was taking a nap while her 8-year-old son was playing in the living room. As the boy was playing, a van crashed through the picture window. The boy was surprised but unhurt. The mother raced into the living room and screamed out the name of her son. With a trembling voice the boy replied, "But Mom, honest, I didn't do it!"

Mother's body is his first information system. If she holds and cuddles him, he feels safe and satisfied. If she is tense or unhappy, he is filled with fear and a general uneasiness. Mother continues to have enormous power over his life well into adulthood, because her most important lessons are taught through primal body language before the age of reason. It's as though she installed within him at birth a software program that she is capable of accessing at any time. This internal program remains etched in the male psyche and continues to shape his perceptions and feelings well into adulthood.

A middle-aged woman made her way into an apartment building to the twelfth floor. As she arrived at her intended destination, she rang the doorbell impatiently. The door opened mysteriously, and she was welcomed by the smell of incense. She entered and was greeted by a pretentiously dressed young girl who announced her presence with the sounding of a huge gong.

With this the young girl said, "Do you wish to see the all-knowing, all-powerful, the wonderful one, Maharishi Narru?"

"Yeah," replied the middle-aged woman impatiently. "Tell Sheldon his mother is here!"

A male infant catches the first glimpse of himself through the reflections in his mother's eyes. Later he'll subconsciously transfer that power to other women in his life. It is as though all women have been given the access code to his psyche and self-esteem. But few future women in his life will wield

Since the Industrial Revolution the powerful father figure in the family has basically been replaced by mom.

the awesome power of his mother. He will perform for them because he first performed for his mother. He will fear their disapproval and seek their confirmation just as he first feared his mother's disapproval and sought her confirmation. Looking into the eyes of his current companion, he may still be seeking the nod of acceptance from his mother. Some men even marry their mother, although she's encased in another woman's body.

Since the Industrial Revolution the powerful father figure in the family has basically been replaced by mom. In an agrarian society, dad was usually nearby as the families worked the fields together. Today dad is no longer present to teach his son how to become a man. The missing father figure has created a vacuum in family relationships that moms have filled by default. Dad belongs to the world of work; mom belongs to the world of family—even if she works outside the home. Sons may even become the surrogate husband to replace the missing father figure in some families. He becomes the listener, the helper, and the "man" of the house.

The son of an absentee father may begin to view mom as almost omnipotent. She's able to work outside the home, manage the household, provide for his daily needs, and even care for him when he is sick. One grown son commented, "The most remarkable thing about my mother is that for 30 years she served the family nothing but leftovers. The original meal has never been found."

Because dad is seldom home to accomplish any of these important childhood tasks or even to listen intently when needed, the son begins to depend more and more upon his mother to define the word "relationship."

The cartoon strip *Momma* portrays the son running up and saying, "Hi, Momma! Can you sew on this button, in a hurry? And iron these slacks? And give me a cold glass of water? Thanks, Momma. Got to run."

Momma looks lovingly at the retreating figure and sighs, "In the Indy 500 of life, mothers are the pit stops."

A son eventually finds himself torn between two worlds—the world of men and the world of women. He often hears other men make derogatory remarks about women, and some even perpetuate the myth that females are inferior to males. This dichotomy between the male mythology and loyalty to mom may cause confusion in the emerging adult male. What is his rightful place in society?

Some first-grade students were asked to come to the front of the class and tell the others what they were going to be when they grew up. One little girl said she was going to be a nurse. Another said she was going to be a doctor. In each case the class seemed suitably impressed.

Then a little boy got up and said, "When I grow up I'm going to be a lion tamer. I'll have lots of fierce lions. I'll walk into the cage, and they'll roar." As he looked at the class for a response, he could plainly see that just about nobody believed him. He recovered his momentum quickly by adding "Of course, I'll have my mother with me!"

This dependence upon mom may create in some men a fear of commitment to any other female. Many men make a sharp distinction between accountability on the job and commitment in a personal relationship. Society expects men to work and be successful. Responsibility and commitment are a given. Apparently our male culture encourages men to be noncommittal or to at least keep their emotions hidden. Perhaps that's why some men feel that the best way to save face is to keep the lower part of it shut. Mark Twain once remarked, "A mother understands what a child does *not* say."

Men who guard against feeling vulnerable in an adult relationship may turn back to mom. She is safe and requires no outward commitment from him, since she has been totally committed to him since he was born. Mom will never reject him or make him feel abandoned as his absentee father will. To guard against the feeling of abandonment, some men never become intimately involved with anyone. They don't share their thoughts and intimate feelings, lest their partner might use it against them at a later date. By keeping themselves busy with career, sports,

> *Many men make a sharp distinction between accountability on the job and commitment in a personal relationship.*

and hobbies, the average man can successfully deny his loneliness—for a time.

Most men don't understand themselves, but they want others, especially women, to understand their needs. Comments received during a men's seminar indicate the male's deep-seated need to be understood.

"Women don't understand that sometimes we want to go fishing rather than be with them."

"Women think we're angry with them if we want to relax by watching TV or participating in sports. They don't understand that we need to be with other men."

"Women don't understand our need to achieve in a career or how deeply that need is rooted in our being."

"Women don't think we feel deeply, just because we fail to express it as they do."

"A woman doesn't understand a man's world. She looks at him through her eyes, and that messes up the picture."

It is not possible to establish an intimate relationship apart from time spent together. The missing ingredient in many families is father spending time with the family.

A man may become very self-centered and unable to expand his circle of care to include another person because he still expects everyone to focus on him as mom did. Some children feel abandoned when both parents are away at work all day and have no idea what they are doing. In addition, many parents divorce, and the mother typically receives custody. Where does the male child find a role model when father is removed from the family?

Intimacy between men is still uncertain or even frowned upon in many parts of our society. Consequently, some men today aren't intimate with anyone, including themselves. This drives some frustrated men even deeper into the consoling arms of mom. Surveys indicate that most sons feel closer to their mothers than to their fathers. The American man may cherish his family, but his children (especially his sons) are more attached to his mate.

● ● ●

God specifically warns husbands not to be so involved outside the family that they neglect responsibilities at home (1 Tim. 3:4; 1 Peter 3:7). He makes it clear that a husband's responsibility within the home extends far beyond material provision. God directly commands the husband to love his wife in the same manner that Christ shows His love for the church (Eph. 5:21-33). It is not possible to establish an intimate relationship apart from time spent together. The missing ingredient in many families is father spending time with the family.

God created males for relationship. Men actually find their reason to exist in relationship. Life's deepest joys are found through relationship. Masculinity is defined in relationship. So why are many men afraid to commit to a relationship? In order to become a man, a male child is taught to develop a sense of distance between himself and the world. He must separate himself from his feelings so as not to be distracted by those around him. Vast numbers of men learn to steel themselves against their feelings about fellow human beings so that as soldiers they can maim and kill. What many male children are taught about manhood detracts from their ability to sustain an adult relationship—except with mom. That relationship was put in place long before they knew about "manly" things. They owe their very existence to mom, and that relationship exists apart from their masculinity. She stands apart from all other women.

Perhaps the influence of mom upon most men can be summed up with the following story.

It was one of mom's most hectic days. Her small son, who had been playing outside, came in with his pants torn. "You go right in, remove those pants, and start mending them yourself," she ordered sternly.

Sometime later she went in to see how he was getting along. The torn pants were lying across the chair, and the door to the cellar, usually kept closed, was open. She called loudly and sternly down the stairs, "Are you running around down there without your pants on?"

"No ma'am," came a deep-voiced reply. "I'm just down here reading your gas meter."

We smile at the influence of mothers over men. However, the Bible clearly states that it's the relationship of husband and wife, not mother and son, that is to be "one flesh." The most intimate relationship on earth is to be shared with a marriage partner, not a parent. A mature one-flesh relationship is what God intended for men and women to experience in marriage.

An adult son describes his own feelings as he viewed that kind of relationship between his parents: "We were watching TV one night—Mom, Dad, and I. The story was without interest, but it served at least to gather us together in the warmth of our living room.

Quietly we enjoyed one another's presence, not bothering really to say much, but just being happy together. Each was lost in his or her own thoughts, and the long day's weariness began to take hold.

"On impulse, I looked toward my father and noticed him gazing lovingly at my mother. Her head was bowed in sleep, and her glasses rested precariously on the tip of her nose. The years, though kind to her, still had left their mark, and her fresh beauty that I marveled at when I was a boy now lingered on, more as a loving memory than a living reality. She seemed so fragile to me, more of heaven than of earth, more of spirit than of substance.

"Dad never took his eyes from her, and I asked him what he was thinking. Slowly he turned toward me and said in a voice that only old lovers use, 'Look at your mother, son. Isn't she beautiful? Really beautiful?'

"'Yes, Dad,' I answered. 'You're right; she is really beautiful!' At that moment I felt like an intruder. What right had I to share this moment of profound intimacy between this man and the only woman in his life? The look of love, tinged with just a trace of sadness, that he directed toward her mirrored years of living together, of whispers and shouts, of certainty and doubts, all mingling and becoming one in the crucible we call love. She would always be beautiful to him because now, through the prism of the years, he could see only her soul; and a lover's soul, as everyone knows, never grows old . . . only more beautiful.

"After a few moments he rose from his chair, lowered the TV, hugged me warmly, and then went over to his wife. He touched her cheek ever so gently and tenderly kissed her good night. At that moment I became overwhelmed with a feeling of gratitude toward God, who chose me to be born of such a love. And I am certain that when the time comes to present his bride, and my mother, to God on Judgment Day, my father's words will be: 'Here is my wife, dear God. Isn't she beautiful, really beautiful?'

"God will agree, and I will respond, 'Hi, Mom!'" (Richard Delisle, *While My Mother Sleeps*).

CHAPTER 5

━━━━ ►◄ ━━━━

Man Talk

No naked lights!"

Now, that was an interesting sign! Ingrid and I (Marvin) had just moved to Hong Kong and were taking an afternoon walk up in the Tai Tam Reservoir when I saw it. I speak English relatively well, but I still wasn't sure what to make of this warning. Upon inspection I saw that it was on the cage surrounding a petroleum tank and figured out that the sign meant "No open flames!"

A few days later I encountered another sign, which read: "Do not enter box unless your exit is clear!"

Hong Kong has rather heavy traffic. This sign was posted at every intersection with a traffic light. The portion of the street that formed the intersection was painted with a bright-yellow box. The English translation? "Do not stop in the intersection."

Simple, huh? You just have to understand the British culture, which has "petrol" instead of "gasoline," "lifts" instead of "elevators," "flats" instead of "apartments," and "bonnets" where your hood ought to be. I really thought I had the hang of it until I read the sign attached above every toilet in the hospital where I worked. "Do not stand on the toilet seat!"

Whether you're married, single, divorced, or have taken a vow of celibacy, you're still going to have to communicate with men at some point in your life.

Now I was confused. You see, I understood the words and their meaning quite clearly. The problem was that I couldn't think of any possible reason I might be tempted to break the rule (or the toilet seat). The problem was that I had to adjust to not one but two or more new cultures.

While in my 49 years of being potty trained I have never once tried it while standing on the toilet seat, I came to realize that Chinese toilets are built considerably closer to the ground. In fact, they are *in* the ground. As a result, many of the local patrons were much more comfortable in a position that required the breaking of the above rule. (By the way, doctors will confirm that the Chinese have a much healthier position on the matter.) I was forced to adapt to their customs on several occasions and never really had a problem except when I was on the train to Beijing.

Most men can't—and don't want to—speak from a feminine culture, but they recognize that in order to speak well, it would be helpful to understand that culture a little better. Likewise, you may begin to understand what your man is trying to tell you if you understand the masculine culture a little better.

Something about the rocking motion challenges one's concentration.

By now you are wondering just what this chapter is about. Actually it's about communication.

Communicate: "To transmit information, thought, or feeling so that it is satisfactorily received or understood" *(Webster's Collegiate Dictionary* [tenth edition]).

When dealing with people from another culture information, thoughts and feelings are received but easily misunderstood. You don't have to cross an international border to experience this phenomenon. Just talk to your teenage children. Talk to your parents. And yes, talk to your Mr. Right.

Whether you're married, single, divorced, or have taken a vow of celibacy, you're still going to have to communicate with men at some point in your life. Before you attempt it again, remember this important fact: Men and women are not exactly alike. You may wish to argue that point with me, but I can assure you that it is now an established fact. Men think from a different perspective. And they communicate from a male culture.

John Gray has written a wonderful book entitled *Men Are From Mars, Women Are From Venus*. He begins by having us pretend that the Martians (men) discovered the Venusians (women), and they fell totally in love with each other. Everything was wonderful until they moved to Earth, and somehow both forgot that they were from different planets. Wouldn't it be wonderful if we could rediscover, accept, and even appreciate the differences that God built in at Creation? We speak different languages. I don't want my wife to learn to speak masculese; I just want her to understand it. This will require time and some deliberate effort on her part.

This chapter and this book in general are written primarily for women who are seeking to make their good relationships even better. If you are already into a difficult relationship, learning to communicate more effectively may not be enough to resolve all your problems, but it is a necessary first step. You may wish to see a professional counselor who can translate what your man is saying.

I'm coming from the position and assumption that your man (husband, father, son, brother, friend) really does love you. If that is not the case, then this is probably not the book to help you with that relationship. (But thank you for buying it anyway, and we hope it will help you understand masculese better for the other men in your life.)

Men want to express love. Men also want to communicate. However, they want to do it in masculese and not feminese. Most men can't—and don't want to—speak from a feminine culture, but they recognize that in order to speak well, it would be helpful to understand that culture a little better. Likewise, you may begin to understand what your man is trying to tell you if you understand the masculine culture a little better. The plea of many men is "Help us talk to you!"

Talk to Him

A satirical statement that I heard many years ago went something like this. "There are no frigid women, only clumsy men." I guess that bothered me. I wondered if it was funny or true. It can't be both. I asked myself then, and I continue to ask myself now even as I write these words today, "Am I a clumsy man?" Am I some kind of sub-human oaf trying to make delicate gestures of affection toward a perfectly formed woman? There have been times when I've felt that way, but most men don't really want to remain that way. They may give that appearance at times, but that is primarily because their male culture has taught them to protect themselves from harm by blocking their emotions. In truth, even as you may long for a gentle man, most men long for a gentle teacher.

Tell your man lovingly what pleases you, how you want things done, and what you find romantic. Tell him how and when you like to be touched. If you don't spell it out, it may take him a long time to figure it out.

How well does a child learn by being yelled at and told that he's stupid when he gives a wrong answer, or worse yet if he's ignored because he has misspoken too often? Learning is much faster when accompanied by praise for things done right (or at least a good honest attempt), rather than scolding or abandonment for missing the mark. Even dogs know that.

What are we talking about exactly? Tell your man lovingly what pleases you, how you want things done, and what you find romantic. Tell him how and when you like to be touched. If you don't spell it out, it may take him a long time to figure it out.

We used to have a sign in our kitchen that read:

I KNOW YOU BELIEVE YOU UNDERSTAND
WHAT YOU THINK I SAID,
BUT I AM NOT SURE YOU REALIZE THAT
WHAT YOU HEARD IS NOT WHAT I MEANT.

When Ingrid and I were having a discussion that was getting nowhere fast, we would just point to the plaque and acknowledge that I was from Mars and she was from Venus.

Women tend to drop subtle hints rather than simply say what they want, because they love it when a man is able to see what they want or need and supply it without their having to ask for it. That's great, except that men tend to be direct and confrontational and often fail to pick up on the hints. I don't see the same things my wife does, or at least not in the same way. A dozen times I'll walk by something that is out of place, and finally Ingrid will say, "Don't you see that? Can't you put it away?" The truth is that I really didn't see it. Or if I saw it visually, it didn't register mentally. She'll purchase a new painting or centerpiece, and I am much more likely to notice it on the monthly statement than I am on the wall or table. Dumb? Not really. Just different.

Men can learn to be more sensitive to changes with a little help. When my wife gets her hair done, it's important for me to notice, although I must confess at times that I don't. However, I've never missed it when she appears in a new negligee.

Don't be afraid to be more open about the things you want from your man. You are not teaching him how to be a man. You are

Women are more likely to want to talk something through, whereas men are more likely to want to think about it awhile.

teaching him how to be *your* man. Not many men would balk at spending time with a willing, eager, sensitive teacher. However, be careful that your honest communication does not make him feel that he's a failure, especially in the sexual arena. Sex is undoubtedly a man's most vulnerable point. Handle his sexual ego with care, just as you want to be handled with care.

I have always found that a little humor makes the learning easier. Ingrid and I will never forget an incident that happened while we were living in Hong Kong. I had been away in the Philippines for a month, and during that time she had installed off-white wall-to-wall carpet over our parquet floor throughout the apartment. She picked me up at the airport and never said a word about it on the way home. We got off the elevator, opened the door, and I just stood there, certain that we had the wrong floor. She said, "What's wrong, honey?"

"Look at the carpet!" I exclaimed.

She grabbed me in her arms and cried, "Honey, you noticed!"

Give Him Time to Respond

"The biggest challenge for women is correctly to interpret and support a man when he isn't talking" (John Gray, *Men Are From Mars, Women Are From Venus,* p. 67).

Women are more likely to want to talk something through, whereas men are more likely to want to think about it awhile. When she says "Can we talk about something?" his internal response is usually "Yeah, let's hear what you have in mind, but I'm probably going to want to think about it before I commit to anything."

Gray describes this as man going into his cave. Going into a cave is a mental state, but it's enhanced by physical surroundings. Sometimes men have their caves handy. My office is a cave, but my study at home is a real favorite. I can think there. I have all my things. (That's a term that defines a lot of stuff.) I have all my old books (mostly by Dickens) and my pictures. I have my desk and a host of little things that make me think better. If I really need to think something through, I go into my study. I have a strong sense of familiarity, safety, and comfort.

My car is another cave. I spend hours there. (Between 4,000 and 5,000 miles a month.) I listen to hundreds of books on tape, and I have two special attaché cases made to hold cassette tapes that contain a wide selection of entertainment ranging from big band to Gregorian chants, from Jack Benny to Ray Stevens, all depending on my mood and what I want or need to think about. I love my caves.

When I was a boy, I had a real cave in the woods across the street from our house. Another friend and I found it, and we had all kinds of "things" and "stuff" in there. Just thinking about it now, I still get a tingle from the specialness of retreating into its safe and comfortable enclosure.

Consider this letter to the editor of *The Do(o)little Report,* a wonderful newsletter dedicated to answering the universal question "Why can't a man be more like a woman?"

"I'd like to know why some men take the newspaper in the bathroom. Why can't they do their thing and be gone? My husband takes a book, magazine, or newspaper in the bathroom, and it's like he has a party. I know I'm in trouble when this happens. Talk about ladies taking a long time to get ready! Ha! Not in my house. The bathroom is his cave!" (vol. 1, No. 6, p. 2).

Why, I think she's got it! The bathroom is frequently a man's cave. What better place to secure privacy in order to contemplate and think things through?

"Women have a lot to learn about men before their relationships can be really fulfilling. They need to learn that when a man is upset or stressed, he will automatically stop talking and go to his 'cave' to work things out. They need to learn that no one is allowed in that cave, not even the man's best friends" (Gray, p. 69).

> *Don't demand that your Mr. Right open himself up instantly. Allow him some time to process the situation and his options. You'll get a lot more commitment that way.*

This is hard for a woman to understand, because she will instinctively draw closer to others when she is upset. To abandon her man in a time of need seems like betrayal. She wants to talk him through it, and the best way to do that is to ask questions. The problem is that the approach which works best between women will only exacerbate the problem with men. Just give him some time to process what's on his mind. Let him know that you understand his need to pull back temporarily and that you'll talk about it later.

Does this mean a man can't be decisive? Not at all, but it does mean that he prefers to analyze his options first. My wife loves it (my choice of words) when she asks me, "Hon, would you like a hot drink and a piece of kuchen?" (She's German.) Too often I'll get this blank look on my face, and there will be no immediate response. She gets the tiniest bit frustrated at my hesitancy, which she takes as indecisiveness. Actually I'm processing the advantages and disadvantages, the timing, the activities I anticipate engaging in during the next 10 minutes, and other critical concerns.

In other words, don't demand that your Mr. Right open himself up instantly. Allow him some time to process the situation and his options. You'll get a lot more commitment that way. But don't be too surprised if he still doesn't easily tell you about the thought processes that led him to his decision. Rehashing all that is about as exciting as rewriting this chapter when the editor gets done scribbling red ink all over it.

You may be asking "Why can't my man just sit down and enter into a meaningful dialogue? Why can't he just talk to me?" He will. He simply needs to think before he arrives at a decision. Your man also needs to realize that you need to talk it through sometimes. You need to be heard. You want him to listen and to tell you that he cares. Likewise, you need to realize that the man in your life needs to think it through sometimes. He needs to look inside before he speaks. He needs you to recognize that and to support him in it.

Communication takes time. When a woman talks about a problem, a man needs to remember that she doesn't necessarily want him to find a solution and fix it. She might just want him to put down his magazine or turn off the tube and listen. When a man does begin to talk about a problem, a woman needs to remember that he's now making himself much more vulnerable than she does when she talks. If you think his idea is really dumb, it might be better if you delayed expressing that opinion until later. Instead, say something like "Thanks for sharing that with me. I'd like to see how it's going to develop." Some of my really dumb ideas have worked pretty well. (Well, I think I've pulled off one or two.)

Go Ahead, Make His Day

Have you ever watched the look on a child's face when you say "You did an absolutely fantastic job; I'm so proud of you"? Do you get tired of hearing compliments? I don't! Sometimes I like to take Ingrid's face in my hands, look her right in the eye, and tell her, "You're the most wonderful woman in the world. I can't imagine life without you." Do you know what that does for her? I just love the look she gets on her face in those moments. Don't think for a moment that men don't thrive on compliments too.

Whether you're a wife, a mother, a daughter, a sister, a work associate, or just a friend, watch for those magical moments when you can affirm the masculinity of a man you care about. Allow him to be a man. Opening a door, allowing a woman to have his seat, or unscrewing the lid on a pickle jar has nothing to do with male chauvinism; it's merely affirming masculinity. Just as women love to be told they're attractive, so men love to be told they're needed. By the way, men also love to be told they're attractive.

There's an old story that I have used in a variety of seminars. It's called "Johnny Lingo." The story takes place in a culture in which wives are secured by giving cows to their fathers. The girl that Johnny is pursuing is quite plain and very insecure. Her father knows that he will be fortunate to get even one cow for her, but he doesn't want to lose face. Johnny stuns the whole village when he offers 10 cows, an unheard-of price for any girl, let alone this one. They marry and move away. When they return sometime later, she is a completely different woman—beautiful, talented, and full of poise. She became what her husband saw in her. The difference

Opening a door, allowing a woman to have his seat, or unscrewing the lid on a pickle jar has nothing to do with male chauvinism.

was in the value he placed on her. Johnny didn't just see something that the others could not see. He treated her according to the value he wanted her to have. She became a 10-cow wife because he treated her like one.

You can't transform the relationship with your man overnight.

The first time you shower him with affirmation, he may run out to the garage to see just how badly the car is damaged. However, if you consistently treat your man as one highly prized, you may see the man you dreamed of begin to develop. If you want a Mr. Right, offer him first-class treatment. Affirmation has a better chance of success than nagging! I'm well aware that this is a two-way street and that men are frequently at greater fault in failing to affirm their women, but affirmation in a relationship begins with one!

> *If you want a Mr. Right, offer him first-class treatment. Affirmation has a better chance of success than nagging!*

In God We Trust—With Others We Have Secrets

Men have a real problem. They rarely open up on a significant level with other men. They often find a woman to be a better listener when they really do want to open up. The problem, or danger, lies in the relationship that builds as confidence increases. Take care of your man. Be a careful, trustworthy, affirming listener. If you want to make sure that your husband, son, brother, or friend never talks to you again, just laugh at his dreams, put down his plans, or share his confidence with another person. Men frequently will not show their hurt or disappointment. They'll just determine all the more that they can't afford to be vulnerable. If someone else comes along later whom they feel will listen without laughing, dream without demeaning, and befriend without betraying, you are in grave danger of losing your man. I know that men need to understand women's needs and become better communicators from that perspective, but that is not the purpose of this book. Your approach to him may make it more likely that he'll be willing to communicate.

One very personal experience in my childhood I had never shared with anyone, not even Ingrid. After we'd been married more than 20 years, we were lying in bed talking one night, and I suddenly felt the need to share that memory with her. It took me a long time to gain the courage, but at what I perceived to be tremendous risk I finally poured it out. I'll never forget her response. She didn't bat an eye. She didn't seem surprised. She just drew me into her arms, and she's never once mentioned it since.

It wasn't something I needed to ask forgiveness for. I just needed to share it, and I learned that I could trust her on the most intimate level of communication. I learned that my secrets were safe with her, and she won't know until she reads this chapter how much that meant and still means to me. Even then she won't be able to comprehend the personal depth of feeling that night holds in my memory. What if she had laughed? What if she had told me what a stupid thing that was? I wouldn't have been angry. I probably would have agreed. But I would have been wounded deep inside. For certain, I never would have done it again. Thanks, hon.

Don't Fence Him In

Sometimes we tend to categorize or stereotype an entire species. It really struck home one day. When we first moved to Hong Kong I had a hard time remembering faces. I think that's pretty typical. They seemed to look very much alike. One day I was describing an American friend to one of my Chinese colleagues, and he stopped me dead in my tracks when he said, "Oh, don't bother. You Americans all look alike." I almost fell over. How could we all look alike? We had different color hair and eyes. We were all so unique! But he didn't see it. We did have a great laugh over that one.

Men are not all alike, although they have a great deal of commonalty. But the reason women tend to conclude that men are all alike is because they come from a different culture where the feminine mind is perceived to be perfectly logical, something that's not a widely accepted fact in the male culture.

See what I mean? Stereotypes can be a major roadblock to real communication.

When talking with a key woman in our publisher's marketing department about this book, I mentioned that it was intended to be a book for women to help them understand how men think. "Oh," she said, "that should be an interesting pamphlet." Very funny! Very, very funny! Actually, it *was* funny, and obviously she intended it that way. I am sure you've heard more than enough dumb blond jokes, too. Do you know why those jokes are all so short? So that men can remember them.

It is healthy for all of us to be able to laugh at ourselves, but remember that stereotypes can block a relationship's development. Men are interested in more than sex. Real men do cry sometimes, and many of them actually enjoy going shopping with their women. The worst thing that can happen is for us to begin taking generalized misconceptions seriously. Are women really worse drivers? Are they incapable of handling critical business matters because they're emotionally unstable? I plead for balance. Enjoy the humor, but don't take it too seriously; also recognize that each person is a wonderfully unique individual hand-crafted by God. Cultural and sexual stereotypes are dangerous to your relational health!

> *The worst thing that can happen is for us to begin generalized misconceptions seriously.*

Say It Again, Sam

I recall an old song that said something about the lady's lips saying no but her eyes saying yes. Men have used mixed signals as a feeble excuse for abusive behavior while in reality it is no excuse at all. The fact remains that we all need to work harder to make sure the intended message gets through.

I saw a great cartoon recently. It showed a man who had just gotten out of the shower and was eagerly brushing his teeth. He was clearly into getting himself presentable for some happy activity when his wife opened the door and explained, "When I said 'Tonight's the night,' George, what I meant was to take out the garbage!"

Poor George! My heart really went out to him. Mixed signals are a man's greatest barrier to understanding what his woman is really trying to say. When a woman says "Do you want to stop for a snack?" she probably wants to stop for a snack. But if the man isn't hungry, he may just say "No" and keep on going. By the time he realizes that she's upset because he didn't stop, it's too late. If he asks why she didn't just say so if she wanted to stop, she'll insist that he should have been able to figure it out. The rule here is: Don't make assumptions. Ask for clarification.

Not only is this true at home, but it is also vital at work. We live in an age of both political correctness and sexual harassment. It seems that some people are almost seeking to be offended. We all need to be sensitive to other's perceptions, but let's give each other a little breathing room too. Make certain that the other person understands what you want to convey. If you feel offended by a man's statement or actions, ask for a clarification before you slap or sue. It is very easy to assume an attack when none was intended. By the same token, if your man says something offensive, albeit unintentional, he needs to have it brought to his attention, and the EEOC may not actually have to get involved. Men are capable of learning to be better communicators. It may not be easy, but it is worth the effort.

> *Make certain that the other person understands what you want to convey. If you feel offended by a man's statement or actions, ask for a clarification before you slap or sue.*

Do you know how many psychologists it takes to change a light bulb? Only one, but the light bulb really must want to change.

Do you know how many women it takes to change a man? Only one, but he has to believe that you really are his friend first. Then that dim bulb may brighten up!

I'll close this chapter with one more reference from *Men Are From Mars, Women Are From Venus:* "Education theory states that to learn something new we need to hear it two hundred times. . . . Not only do we need to hear it two hundred times but we also need to un-learn what we have learned in the past. We are not innocent children learning how to have successful relationships. We have been pro-grammed by our parents, by the culture we have grown up in, and by our own painful past experiences. Integrating this new wisdom of having loving relationships is a new challenge. You are a pioneer. Expect to be lost sometimes. Expect your partner to be lost. . . . Next time you are frustrated with the opposite sex, remember men are from Mars, and women are from Venus. Even if you don't remember any-thing else . . . remembering that we are supposed to be different will help you to be more loving. By gradually releasing your judgments and blame and persistently asking for what you want, you can create the loving relationships you want, need, and deserve" (p. 286).

Here's looking at you, kid!

CHAPTER 6

Why Did I Marry Him?

I just don't feel alive anymore!" lamented a disgruntled wife. "Somewhere along the line I died. He thinks that the only reason I exist is to supply him with food, sex, and clean shirts. I've got to break out of this coffin."

One of the greatest contributors toward marital disharmony is the natural tendency to be nearsighted, seeing our own problems clearly but failing to perceive the problems of our partner. Marital myopia often focuses upon those things that cause us discomfort but fails to reveal what *we* might do to improve the relationship. When self-interest is the dominant commitment in our life, when we devote more energy to serving ourselves rather than our mate, then marriage will likely become a dangerous mine field in which both partners fear to tread.

Desiring our own good is not sinful in itself. God gave us everything, even our own bodies, and He wants us to take care of what He gave us. However, when we put ourselves at the center of the universe, where God belongs, that becomes sinful.

All relationships, even the best ones, have hard, disappointing moments. When we are treated unfairly, our sinful nature wants to get even. We want justice—or at least our perception of justice—to be administered. In that state of mind we tend to inflict emotional wounds upon our mate.

A woman who was called to jury duty told the presiding judge that she was not qualified to serve, because she didn't believe in capital punishment.

"You don't understand," responded the judge patiently. "This is a civil case involving a man who spent $20,000 of his wife's money on gambling and other women."

Quickly the woman replied, "I'll be happy to serve, Your Honor, and I've changed my mind about capital punishment."

The wounds of men, in some ways, are different from the wounds of women. In marriage, men complain more about sexual frustration, whereas women hurt more because of the lack of sensitive involvement. Sadly, neither men nor women are naturally inclined to give of themselves on behalf of their mate. The truth of the matter is that men and women are *equally fallen* and equally committed to advancing their own interest.

Self-centeredness is a major killer of relationships and marriages. Poor communication, temper problems, unhealthy responses to dysfunctional family backgrounds, codependent relationships, and even personal incompatibility all flow from a common source—self-centeredness.

A couple was leaving a football game in a milling throng of people. The husband, who never displayed any affection in public, reached over and took his wife's hand. She was delighted as hand in hand they walked out of the stadium. Once they had reached the parking lot, she looked up at him, smiling, and asked softly, "You didn't want to lose me?"

Sadly, neither men nor women are naturally inclined to give of themselves on behalf of their mate.

"Nope," he replied matter-of-factly. "I just didn't want to have to look for you."

Someone has said that many girls marry men just like their fathers, which may explain why many mothers cry at weddings.

• • •

In some conservative circles Christianity has been reduced to a joyless moralism, a set of responsibilities that need to be obeyed to demonstrate a regenerated heart. Typical counseling advice to marital problems might include:

"I'm sure it's hard to continue living with someone as mean as your husband, but God requires you to do so—and He never commands without providing enablement."

"It's regrettable that you feel so used and empty. But your role as a wife is to submit to your husband, and knowing that you are obeying God will be your joy."

Although much is correct and good in these responses, they may also represent a joy-killing, legalistic attitude. People who measure holiness solely by externals give little thought to what may be going on in the heart. Passion and joy are lost and grace is obscured when obedience to biblical standards is taught in a way that pressures people to do right in order to gain God's acceptance.

In the name of submission, wives have endured every imaginable form of abuse. Some worry that God requires them to sit still while their husbands beat them. Others push themselves to cooperate sexually even when exhausted in order to avoid God's displeasure and their husband's scorn.

A Christianity that emphasizes rule-keeping instead of relationship cannot tolerate ambiguity or freedom, especially when it comes to a wife's responsibilities.

Their lives are tragically emptied of meaning and joy. A Christianity that emphasizes rule-keeping instead of relationship cannot tolerate ambiguity or freedom, especially when it comes to a wife's responsibilities.

Far more often than many suspect, men have twisted biblical teaching on headship to justify dominating their wives, in some cases literally ordering them about as a master would a dog.

"Wives, submit to your husbands as to the Lord. For the husband is the head of the wife as Christ is the head of the church, his body, of which he is the Savior. Now as the church submits to Christ, so also wives should submit to their husbands in everything" (Eph. 5:22-24).

Does this mean that a wife should fetch a glass of water when the signal is given? or have sex on demand? Did Paul designate that women should be doormats and men power brokers?

A couple was called in by the IRS because of the way they had completed their tax form. "Why did you fail to answer who was the head of household?" the auditor inquired.

"The answer is simple," the husband replied. "We've been arguing about the answer to that question for 17 years. As soon as we agree, we'll answer the question."

Someone once compared partnership in marriage to an old Ginger Rogers and Fred Astaire musical. A really good marriage has the feel of a man and woman blending together into natural movements where individuality is obviously present but really isn't the point. Ginger and Fred were a perfect illustration of partnership. As they flowed effortlessly across the floor in perfect harmony of movement, it was clear that one directed the other, but it was unimportant compared to the beauty of the dance. They moved naturally, effortlessly, as a result of many hours of practice and a knowledge of each other's abilities.

Likewise, every marriage relationship can have a rhythm that can be detected only when God's design for marriage is understood and correctly implemented. The roles of headship and submission are as important to a marriage relationship as they were to Fred Astaire and Ginger Rogers in their dancing relationship. In marriage, headship is what a man does when he is living as a godly man, and submission is what a woman does when she is living as a godly woman. God designed one to lead and one to follow in the marriage relationship. Unfortunately, many marriages today are so far removed from God's original blueprint that both headship and submission are often misunderstood and misused.

• • •

A common complaint from women, when it comes to understanding Mr. Right, is that men need to have a little more *class* and a little less *first*.

A woman had been trying for years to persuade her egotistical husband to put an end to the idea that he and he alone was number one. This man was obsessed with being number one. He never stopped talking about being first in sales at the office and first on the list for the next promotion. He enjoyed playing tennis and golf, but only when he won. He had to be first in line to buy tickets for a game and first to hit the parking lot after the event. Does he sound like anyone you might know?

In any case, this man's long-suffering wife watched with interest one day when he stepped on one of those fortunetelling scales. He dropped a coin into the slot, and out came a little card that read: "You are a born leader, with superior intelligence, quick wit, and charming manner—magnetic personality and attractive to the opposite sex."

> *A common complaint from women when it comes to understanding Mr. Right is that men need to have a little more class and a little less first.*

"Read that!" he exclaimed to his wife triumphantly.

She did. Then she turned it over and replied, "It has your weight wrong too!"

We have all been molded by our culture, family, and even church training. More than that, we have inherited tendencies that tend to determine our direction in life. You cannot transform an egomaniac into a passive observer, or a quiet, reflective man into a bubbly, outgoing one. Ultimatums, nagging, and ridicule are more likely to produce stress than the results you desire.

Sometimes you just have to let your man do it his way.

Sylvia tells how Sam proposed to her. "We had been keeping company for months, and I knew that Sam was very fond of me. But he was so shy it seemed that he'd never get up the courage to propose. Then his mother invited me to dinner. His whole family was present, including an aunt and uncle from out of town. The next day Sam asked what I thought of his aunt and uncle. I told him, 'I like them very much.' He replied, 'They like you very much too. In fact, they asked me when we were getting married.' He paused. 'What shall I tell them?'"

But you can help your partner change by understanding him and his needs. In healthy marriages couples regularly help each other change their attitudes, beliefs, and behavior patterns. But it is done in the spirit of "Let's do this together." The approach must be gentle and loving.

Someone has likened adjustments in marriage to two porcupines who lived in Alaska. When the deep and heavy snows came, they shivered from the cold and began to draw closely together. However, when they got close, they began to stick each other with their quills. But when they drew apart they began to shiver once again. To keep warm they had to learn how to adjust to each other very carefully.

My wife, Karen, and I (Len) have changed a lot during our four decades of marriage. She is no longer the woman I married, and I am certainly not the man she married. Growth and change have occurred because we've "stretched" each other—sometimes rather painfully—and during the process we changed both our attitudes and behavior patterns.

One wife, for example, helped her husband become more thoughtful by pointing out to him how much she admired men who were sensitive to the needs of others. Another wife talked calmly with her husband about her career needs, reassured him of her love and devotion to their family, and got him to agree to her returning to teaching on a trial basis. After six months he was so pleased with her

If you think that marriage ought to be a 50-50 proposition, you'll probably be disappointed at least 50 percent of the time.

renewed vigor and enthusiasm that he completely changed his attitude about her working outside the home.

If you think that marriage ought to be a 50-50 proposition, you'll probably be disappointed at least 50 percent of the time. A professional couple who lived next door to us displayed the ultimate 50-50 marital attitude. When it came time to carry out the garbage, she took one sack and he the other. When they shoveled the walk, she did one side and he the other. But their most fascinating (at least for us) challenge came when they decided to spade up a garden spot in their backyard. It was interesting to watch the argument that ensued when he turned over more shovelfuls of sod than she. Eventually he agreed not to put his shovel in the ground until she had completely turned over her shovelful of sod!

The problem with a 50-50 marriage is that you may feel that you're giving more than 50 percent of the time, and eventually you begin to resent your husband's not taking care of his 50 percent. If each partner dedicates 100 percent of his or her ability to the marriage, there will be a lot less resentment and a lot more heavenly harmony. In counseling couples who disagree on household assignments, I often say "The job belongs to the one it bothers the most!"

Karen and I have found that this policy eliminates much of the complaining and bickering in marriage. For example, if it bothers me that the sink is dirty, I clean it. If it bothers Karen that the sidewalk is covered with leaves, she rakes it. Rather than nagging each other about when a task will be accomplished, it's easier to do it oneself.

Marriage should make life easier—not more difficult.

When you stop viewing work as "his" and "hers," there is no limit to how much can be done. We find that we get a lot more done and a lot less said—that later needs to be retracted—when we don't waste time arguing over who should perform a specific task.

Perhaps you are worried that your husband may not perform *any* household tasks because their not being done bothers you more than it does him. If so, try leaving a task undone that you'd normally complete. For example, if laundry is your usual task, try leaving his socks on the floor and his underwear in the hamper until he runs out. If you cannot permit yourself to leave a certain task undone, then the job belongs to you!

Marriage should make life easier—not more difficult.

One potential problem that often exists in modern families is the *superwoman syndrome.* Traditional families of the past always involved division of labor. They complemented each other. The entire family functioned as a miniature economy, with each person dependent on the other for survival. No one tried to "do it all."

However, many women today try to "do it all!" They see men as being able to devote themselves fully to education and career development and still function as husbands and fathers. What women fail to realize is that the only reason men have been able to "do it all" was because they had wives! Women today are trying to "do it all" at work as well as at home. It simply is not possible.

The man who tries to have some kind of balance in his life—be attentive as a husband and devoted as a father—will usually not be a high achiever in his career. Each day has only 24 hours, and time taken away from the pursuit of a career and devoted to family matters will usually shorten the distance traveled on the career track. Men or women who attempt to master the three areas of work, marriage, and family usually end up exhausted, frustrated, and often divorced.

The mandate that men have been given historically is to achieve in the workplace. If a man feels he is doing that well, he is likely to feel little guilt if the price tag includes evening meetings, business trips, and missed activities with his children. Women, on the other hand, tend to get caught up in the bind of working, coming home, and shouldering the responsibility of more than their share of household tasks in addition to maintaining a career. Women can't juggle all these well because the responsibilities are physically impossible to juggle, and so they tend to feel guilty, unlike their male counterparts.

It's important for both husband and wife to assess their values and priorities. You have only so much time and energy, and you should spend it on your highest priorities. There is no way that men or women can accomplish "it all."

Another source of contention in marriage is real or perceived *needs.* Counselors often suggest, "Tell your husband what you need from your marriage." This approach implies that communication will result in change. A word of caution: While communicating your needs may be reasonable as a starting point, it doesn't mean that what you want is something your mate can provide. The underlying assumption is that if your husband truly loves you, he will display superman type efforts to transform himself into the exact model you desire.

If you're married to a *neatnik,* don't expect him to be comfortable if you have sloppy habits. Men and women have been led to believe that change or growth is easier than it really is. Before you make a list of desirable changes you'd like to see in your husband, first make a "for better or worse" list. Acceptance does not mean you have to live with conditions in your marriage that you find irritating or even intolerable, but it does mean that your mate must feel confident that you love him despite any flaws.

One man commented: "I don't want my wife to see me either as a superman or a jerk but as a flawed, struggling person—capable in some areas and incompetent in others, as vulnerable in my way as she is in hers."

> *Acceptance does not mean you have to live with conditions in your marriage that you find irritating or even intolerable, but it does mean that your mate must feel confident that you love him despite any flaws.*

If you equate love with change, you will be consistently disappointed and disillusioned with your marriage. If you didn't like the man you married, why did you marry him? If you liked only 75 percent of him, then your response to the preacher should have been, "I do—75 percent of the time." If you find yourself constantly nagging, criticizing, or feeling irritable whenever your husband exhibits unwanted behavior, you may have a problem with acceptance and need to develop a "for better or worse" list that will let him off the hook.

Josh McDowell offers an interesting bit of advice: "The golden rule of a successful marriage: Whatever qualities you desire in a mate, develop first in yourself."

Few men intentionally set out to annoy or disappoint their wives. Most men truly want to please their partners. Disappointment is upsetting not only to the one who feels it but also to the one who causes it. As one man revealed with great sadness: "My wife is constantly nagging me to talk about my feelings. She says it makes her feel lonely because she doesn't know who I am. The truth is, I don't really know how to express my feelings. I have them, I guess, but I just can't seem to let them out. I can remember as a kid being much more emotional, but my father kept calling me a 'big baby.' Eventually it was just much easier to keep my mouth shut and not let the feelings out."

Romance is often a disputed state in longtime marriages. What happened to the feelings of closeness, ecstasy, longing, and idealization? What happened to the oneness that you once experienced in your relationship?

Perhaps you equated infatuation with love. No matter how wonderful we feel, the truth is that romance is based more on fantasy than reality. Romance is more about what we project into the situation than about what is actually there. It is based on mystery, fantasy, hopes, and desires. Romance dims our eyes to our lover's faults and magnifies his virtues. Eventually

The froth of romance cannot sustain any relationship throughout a long period of time.

the romance lenses are put into our eyes with less frequency, and we begin to see all our lover's faults.

A harried husband remarked, "I want a wife whose love for me is based on the me I know myself to be, not the 'wonderful' me in her imagination. I don't want to have to live up to her romantic fantasies of me and her image of me as being different from other men. I'm bound to fail when I try to live up to that, and I'm sure to disappoint her."

Romance evolves into something more real and substantial called love. While it is less intoxicating, it nevertheless provides a solid foundation upon which to build a relationship. The froth of romance cannot sustain any relationship throughout a long period of time. Love, based upon information and experience, takes over where romance leaves off.

While romance often leads to love and marriage, it doesn't automatically follow that love leads to romance in marriage. Love is about loyalty, fidelity, and companionship. It is about shared dreams, tenderness, and sexuality. Passion's flame flickers at times but burns brightly at other times. Romantic interludes are delightful in any marriage, but not essential for love. Romance is not automatic simply because two people love each other. If you want to keep the romantic flame burning in your marriage, it requires determined effort and planning.

• • •

One assumption about love leads to more difficulty in marriage than almost any other—the notion that when someone loves you, he will almost intuitively understand you. Since most men are predominantly left-brained, intuition is not usually high on their list of available qualities. Women, on the other hand, utilize both sides of their brains with greater efficiency and seem to possess more intuitive ability.

Men in therapy often complain that their wives expect them to be mind readers. "You should have known that would hurt me!" is often the tearful wife's reply. No, he should not have known that would hurt you. That assumption will cause you to experience a great deal of grief.

One man in counseling lamented, "Why can't my wife come right out and tell me what she doesn't like about our relationship and also what specific alternatives we can work on together? I don't want to have to read her mind or come up with solutions that make her happy. It's not enough to be told what doesn't work. I need to know what *does* work!"

As the years go by, most of us have a long list of feelings, needs, and concerns that we've long ago stopped putting into words, believing that they are obvious to our mate. Wrong! It can be helpful and informative to write out periodically such a list and then talk about it with your partner.

One woman was surprised when the top item on her husband's list was "I know I love you, love." Susan didn't know that at all. In fact, it had been a long time since she had heard him say it. "But," he protested, "I thought you knew it, because I've been faithful, we have a pretty good sex life, and I keep coming home to you day after day." He believed his actions expressed his love for her. She needed to hear the words on a daily basis to allay her normal doubts and insecurities.

No matter how much love we may feel for our spouse, nonetheless we often do not detect many feelings and wishes. The wife who is preoccupied with children and juggling her own career may not quickly sense that her husband has had a tough day, and that's normal. Likewise, the husband who comes home and greets his wife, who has been talking to the schoolteacher about their child's performance, may not want to pick up her cues to talk. Instead, he turns on the television to watch the news. Does that make them selfish? unloving? No, just preoccupied and human.

Don't automatically assume anything. Help your husband understand you, and above all, give up on any fantasy about an all-knowing and intuitive mate. Be clear in expressing what you feel and what you need. Your mate may not respond with joy, but at least you will no longer be relying on mind reading.

● ● ●

I often hear women complain, "I just don't feel fulfilled in our marriage."

My initial response is often "Whose responsibility is it that you feel fulfilled?"

Personal fulfillment is always our own responsibility throughout life. Fulfillment is an attitude, a feeling, a conclusion we come to about our current state of growth and well-being. It's

Marriage was never meant to be the antidote to personal difficulties or dissatisfactions, yet many of us expect it to assume that position in our lives.

never something that is provided by another person, however intuitive or well-intentioned that person may be.

Unfortunately, our marriage partner is often the easiest target for any kind of vague dissatisfaction we may feel. Marriage was never meant to be the antidote to personal difficulties or dissatisfactions, yet many of us expect it to assume that position in our lives. We continue to blame our mates for our own problems. If we're depressed, it's their fault. If we had a bad day at the office, it's their fault. If we're spending too much money and cannot stay within our budget, it's their fault. If our sex life is lousy, it's their fault. If our marriage isn't vibrant and alive, it too is their fault.

Feeling fulfilled is the result of what we do for ourselves, not what someone else does for us.

The truth is, it is a whole lot easier to blame someone else for something that is not quite right than it is to look inside and realize that we are the only ones who ultimately can change our experiences. Making someone else responsible for our fulfillment also leads to another predictable outcome: guilt.

Since no one really can fulfill anyone else, most marriage partners feel some sense of guilt at having let down their mates. This kind of guilt never brings us closer to our mates. Instead it drives a silent wedge between because it brings with it feelings of resentment and a wish to retaliate.

When we are not feeling fulfilled, the problem is not necessarily that something is wrong with the marriage. There may be something wrong with how we view our quest of happiness. Feeling fulfilled is the result of what we do for ourselves, not what someone else does for us. Your Mr. Right can be a companion on your journey to fulfillment, but he cannot be the ultimate source of gratification.

• • •

If husbands and wives have one prevailing wish, it is to be friends for life. Unfortunately, men and women who are about to marry seldom know how to sustain a marriage. Their erroneous assumption is that love will take care of everything. The truth is that unless you define love in terms of friendship, your marriage may never experience its true potential. Is your husband your best friend? Are you his best friend? What are friends?

All friendships share certain qualities, such as trust, caring, confidentiality, willingness to give, and fidelity. As the friendship continues, it is strengthened by the knowledge that you have invested much and that it has provided many rewards. You rejoice in your shared history and fondly recall nostalgic reminiscences. You plan and dream together for the future and feel comfortable knowing that your friend will be there to share it with you.

Friends may argue, offend each other, let each other down, have falling-outs, even go through times they have less frequent contact. Friendship between husbands and wives provides an even deeper and more meaningful experience because of the complex element of sexual bonding.

A struggling husband tried to describe his idea of an ideal wife as "a woman who will fight it out with me and, when we argue, try to see our differences as a part of a struggle to get closer, not as something bad that damages the relationship because I've expressed my conflicts about them."

Friends cherish their sense of equality, and the bond of mutual trust that develops

Most men are reluctant to give up traditional gender roles for fear of being seen as less masculine and self-reliant.

encourages freedom of expression. However, there are two major threats to any friendship, especially the friendship of marriage.

Selfishness. This can destroy a friendship as quickly as a marriage. Married couples are often more selfish with each other than they are with their other friends. To remain friends, we must reach out to each other, look for areas of common interest, and put energy into events that our partner considers meaningful.

How often do you do some of the things your husband particularly enjoys? Friendship is the by-product of shared experiences. If you don't share experiences, the friendship will fade.

Stereotypes. Most couples are burdened to some extent by cultur-ally conditioned gender stereotypes. There seems to be an unconscious fear that abandoning these stereotypes will result in our being less at-tractive to our partner.

Most men are reluctant to give up traditional gender roles for fear of being seen as less masculine and self-re-liant. They also have a fear that if they ac-knowledge and en-courage their wife's strength, she will be-come less feminine in their eyes and they less masculine in hers.

Friedrich Nietzsche once said: "It is not lack of love but lack of friendship that makes un-happy marriages."

A newlywed couple had just returned from their honeymoon, and wishing to impress his bride with the importance of cooperation, the young husband threw one end of a rope over the roof of their house and instructed his wife to go around and pull the rope to the ground. Since he maintained his hold on the rope, they both pulled in opposite directions, and nothing was accomplished. Calling a halt, the young man made his way to his young wife's side, and showed her how easy it was for them to get the rope by pulling together.

"What a perfect illustration!" said his wife. "And it will remain perfect if you always come around to pull on my side, as you now did."

Women are also restrained by the gender roles. Many women, despite their conscious wish for a man to be more open and expres-sive, harbor an unconscious fear that their husband will become too needy or emotionally dependent upon them. Therefore, women tend to hide their true strengths from their husbands because they're afraid of being seen as unfeminine.

• • •

Someone has said that "romance talks about love; friendship puts it to the ultimate test." Oddly enough, a major reason husbands and wives are not more companionable is because they unconsciously assume a mate is something different from a friend. While they may view their partner as a lover or a mate, the notion of a friend may be foreign to their thinking. The philosopher Friedrich Nietzsche once said: "It is not lack of love but lack of friendship that makes unhappy marriages."

The following suggestions may help refocus your thinking in the area of friendship:

❤ Respect each other's point of view. There's no right or wrong here; both viewpoints are legitimate.

❤ Evaluate your individual strengths and weaknesses to see what strong points you bring to the marriage and how your spouse balances your weaknesses.

❤ Never assume you know what's going on with your spouse.

❤ Take an interest in each other's topics of conversation and also respect silence.

❤ Seek ways of doing things together that are comfortable for both of you.

❤ Celebrate the tension that differing points of view cause. That tension can enhance your creativity as a couple, giving you alternatives you never knew you had.

Although marital conflicts are common, few are ever fully resolved. They usually are set aside in a kind of uneasy truce, with all the underlying feelings suppressed into the marital underground.

The most common barrier to your husband's becoming your friend is an uneasy regard that he might be the enemy. Although marital conflicts are common, few are ever fully resolved. They usually are set aside in a kind of uneasy truce, with all the underlying feelings suppressed into the marital underground. After this form of "stuffing" has repeated itself during a period of years, most couples cannot even conceive of a genuine friendship based on liking and mutual enjoyment.

A common barrier to friendship in marriage occurs when we confuse friendship rights with marital rights. As husbands and wives, we feel we can make demands on our mate to change this or that trait. At the same time, we want our mate to be our friend, forgetting that friends do not impose such unrealistic expectations on each other. Friends are much more likely to tolerate differences than to request change.

With friends, we are not threatened by differences; we let our friends be who they are. Indeed, the sense of acceptance and understanding we get out of a friendship is what makes it feel alive and comfortable. We like our friends for who they are, not for what we would like them to be.

Clearly, friends are able to give each other honest feedback—perhaps that's one of their greatest values. Friends can allow themselves to disagree heatedly and still feel understood. But all too often in marriage any disagreement is interpreted as arising from a lack of understanding and acceptance. While we do not expect our friends to be mirror images of ourselves, many of us expect our mates to be exactly that.

Women tend to believe that men do not truly value friendship with a woman. They believe that men prefer spending time with their buddies and engaging in more masculine pursuits. It's time to relegate this stereotype to the catacombs of antiquity. Recent studies indicate that 90 percent of married men say their wives are their best friends.

A few years ago it was a commonly held belief that men and women were so different and had such divergent values that they could never be true friends. Although it is true that differences certainly exist between the sexes, it is not true that they cannot trust each other and develop a lasting friendship. An arch is a strength built out of two opposing weaknesses. That is also the secret of a strong and lasting marriage.

> **Recent studies indicate that 90 percent of married men say their wives are their best friends.**

Actually, most married men confess that their only *real* friend is their wife. Many men readily admit that the only person they can rely upon is their wife, and they are deeply grateful. Men typically do not share intimate information with another man. Male conversations tend to stick to sports, sex, and politics. Trust that your husband really wants to be your friend and begin acting on that belief. Husbands *do* wish to be friends with their wives.

Some women are pessimistic about being friends with their Mr. Right be-

> **While it is true that men do not approach intimacy in the same way as do women, they nevertheless want it.**

cause they believe men are afraid of the intimate nature of friendship. It is true that a good friendship requires intimacy, and intimacy requires a close emotional bond that comes from mutual sharing and understanding. Intimacy also requires trust, since it involves sharing our most private thoughts and actions with another person. But intimacy is more than communication. You might share your innermost thoughts, but if they aren't received by your spouse, no bonding occurs. Typically in our society we assume that women are naturally intimate, while men are not.

Many believe that men have a much more difficult time expressing themselves than women. While it is true that men do not approach intimacy in the same way as do women, they nevertheless want it. Because of their deep-rooted fear of being feminized by intimate behavior, most men limit their intimacy to shorter periods of time than women. But this does not mean that men do not wish to be intimate. Men desire intimacy, but women often confuse a man's discomfort with closeness as an indication that he lacks a desire for it. This is a crucial error in logic.

Men will often joke about women wanting love and romance all the time. But the truth is that deep inside, far below the level of conscious awareness, men actually may have more pent-up needs for intimacy than do women. Women who deny or are unaware of this need in men often unknowingly neglect a man's wish for intimacy. As a result, they don't realize how alone he may feel. Most husbands will not talk about this deeply felt need for fear of being humiliated.

A couple's house was filled with plants. The wife truly had a green thumb and enjoyed gardening, but one day she found it necessary to leave town for a week, so she asked her husband to take care of her plants. She gave him specific instructions, ending with the admonition to "please talk to them occasionally."

Her husband, no fan of plants, grumbled that he'd feel like a fool talking to them. When she returned, she found everything just fine, and asked him, "Did you talk to the plants?"

The person who wants privacy does so for his or her own personal needs, not out of a lack of love or a wish to dissolve the relationship.

"No, I didn't!" he answered firmly. "I read the paper out loud in the morning and afternoon, and if they wanted to listen, it was up to them."

One other supposed enemy of marriage is a wish for privacy. Some view this desire as an indicator of a failing marriage. Nothing could be further from the truth. The wish for privacy is one of the indicators marking the transition from the romantic phase of a relationship to the more mature love stage. It isn't necessarily a signal that love is waning. We all have a saturation point; we all need to relax and not have to perform.

Some naively believe that to love someone, you must always enjoy spending time together. Usually the one who craves this closeness feels self-righteous and loving, even as he or she views the privacy-seeking spouse as insensitive and uncaring. Understand that the person who wants privacy does so for his or her own personal needs, not out of a lack of love or a wish to dissolve the relationship. The person wanting more privacy should not be made to feel guilty, yet that often happens.

If you or your spouse desire more privacy, make your negotiations positive and affirmative rather than negative and threatening. If you want more time with your female friends, you can broach the subject by telling your husband what you like about those relationships and what they do for you as a person. Men often take their privacy for granted and yet are reluctant to grant that same privacy to their wife.

Spouses who want to get close to their mates will do so only by changing their own behavior, not their words. If you conduct yourself in a lively and engaging way that promises warm companionship, eventually your husband will have to respond.

If you wish to be a friend to your Mr. Right, see and appreciate what he likes. Do it first. Have patience. You'll eventually find that he will reciprocate. Friendship is action. It happens when we do something to encourage it, when we take a step toward our partner, when we place ourselves, for a time, within the sphere of our partner's needs.

With the world spinning so fast and friendships being so few, a marriage may be the only stable and secure commitment a couple will know throughout their hurried life. It must be put on a higher priority if a person wants to enjoy rest over the long haul. John Fischer, a Christian musician, offers some sound advice along these lines.

John had rented a room from an elderly couple who had been married longer than some people get a chance to live. But even though time had wrinkled their hands, stooped their postures, and slowed them down, it hadn't diminished the excitement and love they felt toward each other. John could tell that their love had not stopped growing since the day of their wedding more than a half century earlier.

Intrigued, the singer finally had an opportunity to ask the old man the secret to his success as a husband. "Oh," said the old gentleman with a twinkle in his eye, "that's simple. Just bring her roses on Wednesday—she never expects them then."

CHAPTER 7

Money—Try to Make the Most of It!

The wealthiest man on the face of the earth is the sultan of Brunei, who has a fortune of $37 billion. Incredibly, the ruler of this tiny Muslim nation admits he's miserable, even though he lives in an $800 million palace complete with 1,876 rooms (including a throne room seating 2,000 people), air-conditioned stables, a heliport, a polo field, 300 acres of landscaped gardens, and a 700-car garage.

He owns 250 fancy cars, but he has nowhere to drive, because nearly every street dead-ends into the surrounding jungle. On the few roads that do go somewhere, the traffic is so slow he can never go fast enough to get out of third gear.

The sultan owns a giant yacht, one of the largest in the world, but he gets seasick every time he gets on board. He has a personal Boeing 727 jet, which he flies in every day, but all he does is make a giant circle and return home. His kingdom is so small that it has only one airport big enough for the plane to land.

He has 22 wives (allowed by Islamic law) who are so jealous of each other that they make his life miserable with constant bickering. To placate them, he built private residences for each one and now sleeps alone and drives his Rolls-Royce to visit each wife. (See Derric Johnson, *Lists, the Book*.)

Money is the number one cause of arguments among couples. People who don't fight about anything else fight about money. People who have been married for 50 years still bicker about it. Money is another one of those topics, like sex, that we don't talk about very well or very often. If you are married, how often do you and your Mr. Right sit down and calmly plan and evaluate your spending and how you feel about it? Do you know exactly what your parents' financial picture looks like and how they have arranged for it to be handled in the event of their death? Do your children know how much money you make and where it all goes? I didn't think so. But if you answered yes to even one of those questions, you ought to be commended and cloned.

The best help I (Marvin) can give you on the subject of money and how it impacts your relationship with the men you care about is this:

1. Don't be afraid to discuss money management.
2. Stay informed. Read.
3. Don't be afraid to ask for help with financial matters.

Aren't the solutions simple? Just talk and read and talk some more, and ask for advice when needed, and all your problems will be solved. Not! Life isn't really that simple. The financial skeleton is found in those three simple steps, but it doesn't have any flesh and blood on it. Steps 4, 5, and 6 put on the

> *We tend to spend a lot of time worrying or arguing about money matters with our parents, children, spouses, and even siblings. It would be better to make a commitment to do something about it.*

flesh and blood that will make a major difference in your life and in the lives of all your Mr. Rights.

4. Take the first step.
5. Take the second step.
6. Repeat steps 1-5 until all parties feel comfortable.

We tend to spend a lot of time worrying or arguing about money matters with our parents, children, spouses, and even siblings. It would be better to make a commitment to do something about it and follow through on that commitment one step at a time.

• • •

One of the most powerful things you can do in your lifetime is teach your children, or your grandchildren, or even perhaps your great-grandchildren, about money. I'll never forget when one of our sons wanted some item that had caught his eye. We explained that we simply didn't have any money for such a purpose. Undaunted, he simply countered, "Then just write a check." Obviously, we hadn't done our job very well. How can you teach children about money, especially in an era of credit card mania?

As soon as your child is old enough to understand some of the basics of finance, include him or her in the process of managing the family budget. This not only will help the child, but will probably encourage you to look at things more clearly and carefully as well. Give your child an imaginary bank account, and each month deposit a set amount into the account. Help him or her learn where the money comes from and where it needs to go.

> **Include your children in family budget planning. Let them see what it takes to make a family function.**

Suppose you give your child $300 each month. Help him or her take out tithe and offerings first. Perhaps that would amount to $45, which would leave him $255. Next, the youngster needs to learn to pay himself or herself in savings. Have him or her deposit $30 into the savings account. It might be appropriate for you actually to deposit that amount in a college account. That leaves $225 to work with. The child's part of the house payment might be $100. Explain that this covers a portion of the principal, interest, taxes, and insurance. It might also include some of the utilities, phone, etc., all of which he or she uses. Your child now has $125. Deduct another $50 for food; $40 for car, gas, and upkeep; $15 for clothing; and $5 for things you do together as a family, leaving $15 for personal discretion.

You can use any figures that seem appropriate in your imaginary budget. Obviously, the amounts are not set and are not really too important, although they should be somewhat realistic. The key is to teach the value and use of money. I also strongly encourage you to instruct your children that the money placed in their imaginary account must be earned by accomplishing the work that you assign them. A child who grows up with a system like this will probably apply it when older. I wish I had been as wise when I was younger, but it's never too late to learn better ways. If it is too late to teach your children, then share this information with them so that they can instruct their children in financial matters.

Include your children in family budget planning. Let them see what it takes to make a family function. If you make it an operation that they can participate in, you'll be surprised at how much they will enjoy the learning experience. Encourage them to ask why various expenditures are included. Help them understand that electricity costs money, as do phone calls, trips to the park, glasses of water, and so on. Each expense has to be evaluated and prioritized. Some money can be used "just for fun," but it still must be accounted for.

Take your children to the store with you. Explain why you're purchasing one brand rather than another. Teach them that some sale items are good buys while others are not. Help them understand and develop a value system. Allow them to make some choices, and help them evaluate the outcome of those choices without criticism. A basic rule to remember is: Keep it fun. Expose them to the responsibility of money management, but don't dump on them the pressure you might have experienced from poor planning. I will say, however, that it's good to let them see and learn from some of your own mistakes.

> **The most crucial ingredient in money management training is time spent in communication.**

Teach them where money comes from, how it is made and placed in circulation. Teach them the different coins and bills and how a checking system really works. Help them learn how credit works and show them how it can be a blessing and is necessary for some things (such as housing and cars), but also how it can be a curse if used to purchase items that are not needed or cannot be afforded.

Children think in absolutes. Everything is either true or false. Most children assume that adults always tell the truth. It doesn't last long, does it? Watch commercials with them and help them analyze their purpose. Ask them if they think the product can really provide everything it promises. Teach them to analyze sales tactics and how to look at the whole picture. People in sales and advertising have a job to do, but so does the consumer. You will be absolutely amazed at how fast young customers can become smart money managers. Do not be afraid to let them make some mistakes, and resist the temptation to make everything all right. Let them live with the consequences of their mistakes. Haven't you learned some pretty valuable lessons that way? If you rescue them from all their poor choices now, they'll expect you to do it when they grow older as well.

• • •

The most crucial ingredient in money management training is time spent in communication. You can vary the approach and application a hundred different ways. Talking to your children about money is not too hard. It is one of their favorite subjects, and if you start when they are young, you will find them to be willing participants. Talking to your older parents may be a bit more challenging, especially if there has not been a pattern of open communication regarding finances.

It is not at all uncommon for adult children, upon the death or incapacitation of their parents, to be shocked as they look through the papers that are left. They may find assets that they knew nothing about or indebtedness that is larger than the estate.

Dads who are otherwise first-class have a variety of reasons they don't talk about their finances with their children. Maybe your father is one. These include:

❤ They may feel they haven't handled it all that well themselves and are embarrassed.

❤ Families often don't feel comfortable talking about death. Like sex and money, it is a subject we just don't deal with.

❤ Dads, especially older dads, tend to feel that their money is their own business, and they become protective about privacy.

❤ Believing that their estates will change, they assume that there really is no point in getting involved in a discussion now.

❤ Some dads may be afraid, justifiably or not, that their children will somehow take advantage of them if they know what is available.

Should you bring up the subject? Yes, there's nothing wrong or self-serving in asking to be informed about your parents' plans, holdings, and general financial standing. Assure Dad that you are not seeking an early inheritance, a larger share, or even all the details. You are wanting to know that he does indeed have a plan and that it's properly laid out. You also want to know if there is a safety deposit box or other place of safekeeping that you would not necessarily be aware of. Ask who is going to handle the estate. These are all questions of a general nature and usually are not perceived as probing into private information.

If you're like most couples, you don't spend much time talking about money unless it's in the form of an argument.

If you simply cannot ask him directly, then at least share an article on estate planning with him and ask what he thinks about it. If he has not made adequate arrangements and doesn't want to talk about it, you might suggest to his attorney, physician, or a trusted friend that they bring up the subject.

If you have brothers and/or sisters, make sure that this conversation is a family affair. It would be improper—and possibly even illegal—to do it alone. You may find more hesitancy on the part of your siblings to bring up the subject than from dear old Dad. Work it through together as a family. The time spent in talking will help clear the air, and it will make it much easier to work through the family finances when the parents are gone.

• • •

Now let's look at how money impacts your relationship to your husband. If you're like most couples, you don't spend much time talking about money unless it's in the form of an argument. Furthermore, it doesn't matter whether you have a lot of it or very little. Couples still don't usually talk about how to manage it or how it makes them feel.

Ed and Laura were both in their 30s and were very well established. Neither had been married before, and it was clear to me that they were very much in love. Ed had a good business, and his annual income was in six figures. (Mine is too, but that includes the two numbers after the decimal point! His didn't.) Money didn't appear to be a problem.

However, Ed had a drinking problem, which Laura knew about, and an even bigger gambling problem, which she didn't know about. Losses frequently ran into the tens of thousands of dollars.

One day, a little more than two years after their marriage, Ed hopped on a plane to Reno and lost more than $300,000 before returning home that night. Despondent over his lack of control, he killed himself.

Laura found him a half hour later and called me with the news. The note that Ed left simply asked forgiveness and stated, "I just couldn't talk about it."

No matter how much or how little money is involved, you both must have a clear and open understanding of how much is available and what and where it is going. If one partner is unwilling to discuss it openly, something is wrong in the relationship, and you need help. If your husband tells you that he simply doesn't want you to worry about it, tell him that you'll worry a lot less if you know the facts. Manage and spend your money together. Allocate a specific amount for personal discretionary spending, but let that be an equal figure agreed upon by both of you.

The same basic formula applies here as in so many of the other areas that we have covered. Spend time communicating with each other. How much time? Whatever it takes for both of you to understand and feel good about your finances.

If you find it difficult to get into the subject on your own, agree to read a book together and discuss how you feel about what you read. A number of quality authors deal with family finances from a Christian perspective. Larry Burkett and Ron Blue have books that you can find in most Christian book stores. My personal recommendation are two books released by the publisher of this book: *It's Your Money, Isn't It?* by G. Edward Reid, and *Making Ends Meet,* by

Henry Felder. You can even get a workbook and a video presentation to go along with Reid's book. No matter what source you use, do it and do it together.

We enter marriage as individuals, and money is certainly a key part of our individuality. It embodies such emotions and feelings as power, independence, control, guilt, and security, all of which have a major impact on love. When finances are the root of marital tension, love often suffers. Let me share 10 suggestions that I have gleaned from trusted friends and personal experiences, both good and bad. They are not prioritized, with the exception of number one.

1. Put God first. Practice faithfulness to God in your financial dealings. Return your tithe, give offerings, and believe that God will bless you. "But seek first his kingdom and his righteousness, and all these things will

When finances are the root of marital tension, love often suffers.

be given to you as well" (Matt. 6:33). If you read that verse in its context, you'll see that God is teaching us not to worry about the things that money can provide. Concentrate first on your relationship with Him. Establish the practice of praying together for financial wisdom and about family expenditures. Allow time for God to answer.

2. Test your wants and needs. Impulse buying can appear to be so right, but it often turns out so wrong. Agree ahead of time that you'll wait for a month before making any major purchase. This gives you ample time to evaluate your finances and your real need as well as to do some comparative shopping. If you have to borrow in order to purchase the desired item, you probably do not need it. It's truly amazing how many "needs" we can live without and how many others can be purchased in used, but perfectly acceptable, condition. A 30-day waiting period will help you sort things out.

3. Budget. There is a very simple but effective rule for sound financial management: Earn more than you spend. That's not very profound, but a high percentage of couples don't live by it. Plan together where you want to be financially five and 10 years from now. Establish a pathway to get there based on realistic data, and then walk the path one step at a time. You may have to make adjustments as you go along, but that is a whole lot easier than just walking blindly. To start out, write down everything you spend any money for, no matter how seemingly insignificant. Know where all the money is going. Evaluate your expenditures on a regular basis and make

Choose a home with an eye to resale value. Don't buy one that taps out your budget with the total payment.

cuts where you deem necessary. Follow this plan, and you'll be on your way to financial responsibility.

4. Save. Make sure that your budget includes a specified amount for personal savings. The best plan is a payroll deduction plan so that you never really see the money. At least this is best for weak-willed people like me. It's too easy to feel the pinch of a "need" and skip a payment to oneself. Know and understand the difference between savings, investment, and speculation. Build enough savings to see you through most emergencies. Once you have enough to cover your budget for six months or so, you should begin to invest in some solid and safe growth funds. Speculation is for those who can truly afford to lose all their speculation funds.

5. Consider buying a house. Be prayerful, and then be careful. Make sure that you are buying the right home for your family needs. Don't try to start out with a dream home. It may turn out to be a nightmare. Choose a home with an eye to resale value. Don't buy one that taps out your budget with the total payment. Settle for a little less with potential for improvements that you can do, and pay it off sooner by paying a little extra on the principal each month.

Ed Reid, author of *It's Your Money, Isn't It?* shows how two families purchased a $100,000 home with a $10,000 down payment. One family bought their $100,000 home and financed $90,000 at 12 percent interest for 30 years. Their monthly payments were $925. The other family bought a $60,000 home and financed $50,000 at 12 percent interest for seven years, with payments of $882 per month. At the end of seven years the second couple had paid for the home, with a total outlay of $74,141. They then bought a $100,000 home and financed $40,000 at 12 percent interest for seven years with payments of $706 a month. After another seven years that home was paid for, with a total of $59,313 in payments. At the end of 30 years the first family had paid a total of $333,270 for their home, whereas the second family had paid only $133,454—a savings of nearly $200,000!

Also don't rush into buying. Renting for a period of time will not necessarily set you back. Save for a down payment, and know that you're going to stay in an area long enough to offset the costs involved in purchasing.

6. *Use credit cards wisely.* Believe it or not, there are wise uses for credit card purchases. Many cards offer extended warranties on items purchased, and they will also help settle any disputes that may arise over quality or inaccurate advertising.

If you are using the card, however, because you don't have the cash, you are heading into dangerous water. If you have trouble avoiding that temptation, then destroy your cards and take your chances with the warranties offered by the store and the manufacturer.

Make a hobby out of finding previously owned items rather than buying everything new. Cars aren't the only items that depreciate significantly the moment you take them off the property.

7. *Be thrifty.* Make a hobby out of finding previously owned items rather than buying everything new. Cars aren't the only items that depreciate significantly the moment you take them off the property. My wife, Ingrid, has even found many clothing items of excellent quality at consignment shops. She also uses these shops to sell her clothing that she no longer wears. Many couples enjoy garage

sales or auctions as a form of entertainment. Just make sure that items purchased are previously agreed upon, needed, and in the budget.

Consider buying clothing items out of season. Planning for future known needs can save you a lot of money. Everyone knows that Christmas items are a bargain in January. Why not take advantage of the sales? The spirit of Christmas may be past, but the spirit of saving continues throughout the year. Be thrifty in your food budget too. Buy in bulk when practical, but remember that there's nothing practical about throwing out unused portions of bargains. Many generic or store-brand items are just as good as the so-called name brands. Don't be stingy with variety or quality, just be smart. Plan ahead on food purchases, but don't be so stuck to a week's menu planning that you miss the sale items that won't be around next week.

8. Live on one salary. I know that sounds difficult at best, but read the rest of the story. Budget so that one salary will cover all the truly necessary items to continue normal family functioning. Use the second salary for saving, investing, and miscellaneous expenditures. Then, in case of an emergency your family needs will still be met.

9. Live a little. Keep a little spontaneity in your life. Healthy food choices are important for daily living, but a banana split can do wonders for the soul on a special occasion. Allow for some "mad money," and

Healthy food choices are important for daily living, but a banana split can do wonders for the soul on a special occation.

indulge a whim once in a while. Reward yourself for establishing a budget and sticking to it. If your overall plan does not allow for this, then it needs to be reworked. Obviously you still have to be responsible and look at the big picture, but do stop to smell the roses when you see them.

10. Experience freedom from guilt. No matter what your present situation is, learn from it and go on. Nothing is to be gained by berating yourself over past mistakes or bad habits. Learn, change, and get help if it is needed.

This last suggestion is really important for some couples. If you see that you're developing a disastrous financial lifestyle, get help! Beware of companies that offer to fix everything for you. Some of them are helpful and honest, but many are not. Check with agencies like the Better Business Bureau before you get involved. Most areas have Consumer Credit Counseling services that are offered free of charge. They can help you establish a budget, manage your finances, and even intercede with creditors for you. But you have to take the first step.

> *The truly wealthy person is the one who enjoys living the most. Possessions and bank accounts have little to do with it. Attitude determines true wealth.*

Even Mr. Right is not always easy to talk to about money. Approach your man with caution, but do approach him. Remember this: The only difference between men and boys is the tone of their voice and the price of their toys.

• • •

Wealth and good living include more than money. The truly wealthy person is the one who enjoys living the most. Possessions and bank accounts have little to do with it. Attitude determines true wealth. We all have more than we really need. I have been with people in the squatter's huts in Hong Kong who had a great deal more joy than many of the highly successful businesspeople I've known.

Strive for balance. Live a little. Laugh a little. Love a lot! Spend more time reaching out and touching others. You may even find that it's an inexpensive but truly rewarding form of family time.

Choose to be happy and healthy. Health is more than absence of disease. It involves living with vitality and passion and enthusiasm. I've known many wealthy and healthy people who lived short lives with few amenities. For them it was not a sacrifice, because when the Lord Jesus Christ comes, material things aren't going to matter.

I was asked to officiate at a funeral for a young father who had taken his own life and left a wife and four children. These are never easy funerals. As part of the service I was asked to read letters that each of the children had written to their dad after his death. I knew this was going to be difficult, so I slipped into a private room and read the letters alone. I poured out my tears in private in order to keep my composure during the funeral service. I made it through almost all the letters without breaking down. But the last one written by his 9-year-old son caused me to lose my composure.

"Goodbye, Dad. Thanks for all you did with me. Thanks for playing catch and watching cartoons with me. And thanks for taking me to Cub Scouts. I miss you. I love you. Goodbye."

Even now as I write these words tears fill my eyes. What was important to this young man was not the big gifts or the big trips, but the time they spent together. Use that concept to help you keep a proper perspective in your relationships with your Mr. Right. Planning, frugality, and responsible spending are vital to any family, but they are useless if they are not wrapped up with lots of caring, loving time together.

CHAPTER 8

Lead Him Not Into Temptation

My willpower is strong enough to withstand anything but temptation." So goes an old joke. Just how comfortable are men with talking about their temptations? Perhaps one might answer, "That all depends on which temptations you're talking about." Are you talking about my temptation to eat between meals? Are you referring to my being tempted to call in sick when I really just want to have an extra day off? Or are you referring to my occasional desire to trip the boss when he or she isn't looking?

Such temptations most men will admit to rather easily. Catch your Mr. Right in the right frame of mind, and he may even admit he wants to spend more time at the office than he should. A candid admission of a latent desire to overachieve. Might this be your man?

Most men are reluctant to display openly their truly private thoughts and temptations. Christian men, especially, are too often assumed to have risen above such earthly temptations as lust, anger, and covetousness. As a result of this myth, talking openly about temptations can be a risky step for the men you know. Most likely they don't need any more guilt in their lives. They've piled on enough of their own. That is not to imply that we are trying to whitewash sin or lower Christian standards. We are, however, eager for men— young and old— and the women who love them to recognize the reality of how God made us and how Mr. Right, made in the image of God, should handle temptations.

Whether you're an intimate marriage partner seeking to become one flesh with your man, a concerned mother trying to guide the development of your son, a daughter watching Dad struggle with change, or simply a true and trusted friend, you are vital to helping your man navigate through the mine field of private temptations—not bizarre, deviant thoughts, just average temptations. Knowing some of the areas men commonly battle with may help you to know that he is normal.

What is the greatest weapon in the war against temptations? Many will quickly answer "Prayer," and I (Marvin) agree. "Watch and pray so that you will not fall into temptation. The spirit is willing, but the body is weak" (Matt. 26:41). "Submit yourselves, then, to God. Resist the devil, and he will flee from you" (James 4:7). "Let us then approach the throne of grace with confidence, so that we may receive mercy and find grace to help us in our time of need" (Heb. 4:16).

> **Prayer is a direct link to help, but God often uses human resources as one of His greatest tools.**

• • •

Prayer is a direct link to help, but God often uses human resources as one of His greatest tools. Just as we find our greatest spiritual help from communication with God, so a man's greatest human help is communication with an intimate friend sent by God. What are the attributes that make talking to God comparatively easy? Well, He's always ready to listen and He doesn't interrupt. He doesn't laugh at man's weaknesses (although I believe I've heard Him chuckle over my knuckleheadedness a few times). He's forgiving and understanding even when He is hurt by what we have to share. Perhaps most important, He never betrays confidentiality. He really is a good friend, isn't He?

In His human form, Jesus admitted His own vulnerability and temptations. He became human so that we could know He understood our flaws and temptations. He is an understanding friend.

"Because he himself suffered when he was tempted, he is able to help those who are being tempted" (Heb. 2:18). "For we do not have a high priest who is unable to sympathize with our weaknesses, but we have one who has been tempted in every way, just as we are—yet was without sin" (Heb. 4:15).

He also intimated that He desired human companionship as He

wrestled in the Garden of Gethsemane. Consider, too, His words of anguished confusion on the cross as He cried out, "My God, my God, why have you forsaken me?" (Mark 15:34).

Yes, He was tempted. But He did not sin. Perhaps we could identify with Him more if He had given in just once, but then He could not have been our substitute, could He? You can identify with your man's temptations, can't you? Because you and he are both fully human. You have both displayed a weakness for sin.

Because you can identify with his weaknesses, you can be a compassionate listener. You can choose not to laugh or react in horrified disgust. You can forgive, even when hurt, and you can keep a secret. Furthermore, you can admit to weaknesses and temptations of your own and seek his strength, support, and understanding.

Some temptations are obviously easier to talk about than others. It's much easier to discuss temptations that do not plague our own minds. Most men have never been seriously tempted to commit murder. "Seriously" is a key word. That is not to say that it is not possible, but it's most likely not something your man has wrestled with. Likewise, he has not likely been tempted to rob a bank—not that he couldn't use the money. But there, too, a scenario could develop that might make robbing a bank seem like a good

> **Because you can identify with his weaknesses, you can be a compassionate listener.**

idea. When an individual is desperate enough, the unthinkable may suddenly become an option. Ask the survivors of the Donner party. That doesn't necessarily justify the behavior, but it does illustrate that we really can't judge others until we have walked in their shoes.

So although your man may not have been seriously tempted to commit murder, he undoubtedly has been very angry at more than one person in his life. He may have wished a person were dead. How close does that come to murder? In the Sermon on the Mount Jesus said: "Anyone who is angry with his brother will be subject to judgment. . . . But anyone who says, 'You fool!' will be in danger of the fire of hell" (Matt. 5:22).

Similarly your husband, father, or male friend may never have been tempted to commit adultery. That is, he may never have had to debate the question "Should I or shouldn't I?" He may not have asked, "Could I get away with it?" But Jesus reminds us that "anyone who looks at a woman lustfully has already committed adultery with her in his heart" (verse 28). So, what does it mean to have lusted after a woman? Most men cannot conclusively answer that, but they ought to ask it in their own mind.

According to an extensive survey done by my coauthor among nearly 600 professional caregivers, 65 percent of the males and 31 percent of the females admitted to having been sexually attracted to a client or parishioner without having committed adultery.

Is that good news or bad news? Personally, I'd say it is good news, because it demonstrates that all systems are functioning. I'd also say that each of them would do well to seek a trusted friend's help in evaluating the extent of that attraction and whether or not he or she has worked through the dynamics of such an attraction. Women, and perhaps wives in particular, I am calling you to be such a trusted friend. Interestingly, 45 percent of the men, but only 38 percent of the women, said that they would feel comfortable talking to their spouse about such an issue.

I asked my wife, Ingrid, "What temptations do women struggle with? Do they have lustful thoughts? Would that be an area of concern to women?"

She said, "Of course."

I was behind her and massaging some knots out of her neck and shoulder muscles when I asked; but when she answered, I came around and looked her in the eye and said, "Oh yeah, about whom?"

Her answer? "You tell me yours first."

Now, I'm not so sure it would be a good idea for me to come home every night and list the names of the women I thought were attractive, but I'll tell you it *was* comforting to have her hint to me that she'd be able to understand and identify with such a problem.

What keeps me faithful? First, my desire to strengthen my relationship with God. Second, my desire to strengthen my relationship with my wife. Third, my desire to retain the respect of my children and then my friends. Fourth, my desire to retain the trust and respect of my church. And finally, my desire to retain my self-respect.

But you know what was really helpful and exciting about that discussion with Ingrid? It felt good to be invited into her confidence. She wasn't divulging any dark secrets to me, but she was open for discussion and not put off by the question. Every time she opens the door, I feel just that much closer and committed to her. She was saying, in effect, "We can talk about this."

Let your man know that you too can talk about temptations. Let him know that you struggle with your own. Let him know that you will try to understand his. This is the way to build a first-class relationship.

• • •

What are some of the temptations common among men?

Anger. Anger is certainly not an emotion unique to men, but it is the one expression of feeling that seems to be accepted and expected in males. Men are often tempted to use anger as a cover or an excuse not to deal with the real issues. In a baseball game a batter is called out on strikes. More often than not he'll react in disapproval, disgust, or in outright anger. In any sport when the call goes against him, the appropriate, face-saving reaction is anger, if not outright rage.

> *Let your man know that you too can talk about temptations. Let him know that you struggle with your own. Let him know that you will try to understand his.*

Taking it out on somebody else prevents him from having to deal openly with his own failure. That may not be tragic when that somebody else is the umpire or the referee. After all, they get paid to take the abuse. But when that somebody else is his wife, children, dog, or whoever happens to be in his way, it is quite another matter.

This pattern of passing the blame has a long history. Satan, angry at being cast out of heaven, set out to create doubt in the mind of Eve. "It appears that God wants to withhold something good from you. Not only that, but He lied to you too! He said that eating the fruit from the tree of the knowledge of good and evil would cause you to die. That's nonsense! You will not die."

Eve ate, and it appeared that the serpent was right. She didn't die. "Look, Adam, isn't this fruit beautiful? You should taste this. It's delicious beyond belief."

So Adam ate, and it *did* taste good. But something strange and new came over them. Their very appearance changed. They saw each other's nakedness, and for the first time they felt ashamed.

Later God came walking through the garden and called for His friends, only to find that they were hiding because of their nakedness. He confronted Adam first. And did he own up to his failure and take responsibility

A man is much more easily led by a woman when he's certain of her love and affection.

for his own decision? No! Instead he blamed his lovely fruit vendor. "She fixed dinner, God. That's her job. It's her fault!" He used anger to divert his own responsibility. Blame casting is a form of anger. (Keep in mind that she also passed the blame onto the serpent.)

In the very next chapter things got worse. Blame-casting was passed on to the next generation. Cain and his younger brother, Abel, brought their offerings to God. Abel's offering was acceptable, but Cain's was not. Scripture does not, at this point, give a detailed explanation, but for whatever reason, Cain did not bring a proper offering. He knew it, and God pronounced it unacceptable. Cain was irate. His fury gave the indication that God was wrong. But he couldn't get rid of God, could he? So he transferred his anger to his brother and killed him. To this day men accept—and often admire—brute strength as a logical means of settling what is wrong with the world. As a result, we have hatred, bigotry, and denial.

What can you do about misdirected anger in your man? Acknowledge that you are tempted to react the same way at times. Affirm his strengths. Cautiously and lovingly lead him back to reality and the right path. A man is much more easily led by a woman when he's certain of her love and affection.

Remember also that it is easier to correct the course of the ship once the height of the storm has passed. Don't confront him in his anger. Let it pass for the moment, but don't fail to have that talk when his smile has returned. Try to help him identify the true source of his anger, which might not be the act, word, or circumstance that he blew up over. If that's the case, it may take some time and trust before he will explore it. In order to help, you must first establish an open and trustworthy relationship. Even without such a relationship you can still help by leading him to someone he does trust and has confidence in. If you're truly seeking to understand your Mr. Right, then accept that you do not have to be the one to solve all his problems, temptations, and anger. Just being able to understand them better will help you draw closer to him, no matter what your relationship.

Competition. Competition, like anger, is a big part of a man's life. Many psychologists have proclaimed, "Competition is bad." They often refer to all competitive sports with their blanket statement. However, gaming seems to be universally an important part of the masculine culture. There is no question that it can be—and often is—taken to extreme, but some people have a tendency to throw out the baby with the bathwater. Competition is inevitable. We compete for grades and girls, attention and affection, jobs and justice, as well as a host of other things. Competition isn't bad, but how we handle it and react to it might be.

If competition is a natural and inevitable part of life, then how can it be considered a temptation? Too often it seems to be an attractive shortcut. Competition is not only the way to obtain something, but it may also be the way to retain it as well. The high school sports hero wins the attention of many girls in school. How does he keep their interest? Obviously by competing well. A nonathletic male may be able to compete with a winning car, a full wallet, or exceptional looks. It's a strong temptation to rely on possessions, performance, and appearance rather than relational skills such as communication or just plain caring.

Are men wanting to impress you with what they have or with who they are? A mother may offer profuse praise for accomplishment. A sister may fawn over her brother because he lets her borrow his car to go out with friends. Daughters, friends, and wives all have a variety of ways to reward achievements or perceived advantages achieved by competition. This isn't all bad, mind you, and I'm not suggesting that men unilaterally want to stop the games, but they do need balance in your affirmation to help them not be tempted to give an unbalanced emphasis to competition.

What can you do? Let your men know that you appreciate the things they do and give and achieve but that you love them for who they are. Let them also know that the competition is over. "There's not another dad like you in the whole world." "I'm so proud of you, son, and nothing will ever change that." "Thanks, brother, for being there when I need you." "Sweetheart, I like me best when I'm with you." Words, actions, and time will tell him that competition may be part of life, but it's not the key to being a part of your life.

Sexual attraction. Probably nothing comes more naturally to a man than sexual attraction, and few things can anger a woman more than when that attraction is misdirected.

> **It's a strong temptation to rely on possessions, performance, and appearance rather than relational skills such as communication or just plain caring.**

I confess! I find women attractive, even sexually attractive. I certainly don't apologize for it, and I refuse to say "The devil made me do it," because he didn't. God did. How I and other men handle that attraction is a matter of serious concern. What does this mean for Mr. Rights and the women who love them?

1. Admit vulnerability. In our First-Class Male seminars we are constantly challenging men to admit that they are vulnerable, and we encourage them to accept that fact. Men are attracted to women primarily through vision and secondarily through relationships. Women are attracted to men in just the reverse order. I strongly believe that most men do not view women as sexual objects. However, when a man sees a woman who fits his subconscious criteria for attractiveness, his thoughts may naturally turn sexual.

Provide an atmosphere in which your man can talk to you about his feelings without feeling ashamed.

Christian men will certainly desire to maintain Christ's attitude in their thoughts, and I know that many of them struggle in this area. The very first step, and perhaps the most positive one, is to recognize their own vulnerability and to acknowledge that God created Adam with similar desires. The great difference, of course, is that men are now influenced by the effect of several thousand years of sin. How can women help?

First, you can admit and accept your own vulnerability. This is true whether your Mr. Right is your dad, son, brother, friend, or husband. If we are going to grow in this area, we have to take the undeserved shame out of it. There is nothing shameful about recognizing and acknowledging that a woman other than a wife is attractive. That's like acknowledging that the neighbor's flowers are attractive and beautiful to look at. The problem comes when one decides he needs to pick his neighbor's flowers. That's obviously an overly simplistic comparison, but it makes the point.

A man should not be made to feel shame for feelings of attraction or for sexual drive. Help the men in your life recognize that God gave them both. Provide an atmosphere in which your man can talk to you about his feelings without feeling ashamed.

I always knew that I was vulnerable, but it was something I

wanted to keep hidden. I felt that I should be saying that I wasn't tempted and that those who had committed sexual sins were simply not committed Christians. Now I have seen it happen too many times, and I believe that many of those involved were committed but that they didn't have all the right connections. What a blessing it is to be able to talk and listen to others who can identify with our personal struggles!

The first time I was able to appreciate such freedom was nearly 25 years ago when I finally went with a friend to AA. Because of alcohol I had, at the early age of 24, lost more than one job, a marriage, and most of my hope. In my first meeting I was able to follow the lead of others and say, "My name is Marvin, and I'm an alcoholic."

Their response? "Hi, Marvin."

There I found friends who would accept me, no matter what I had done. The only thing they wouldn't accept was my denial. I was vulnerable to alcohol then. I am still vulnerable today after nearly 25 years of sobriety. The fact that I know I am vulnerable is an important factor in staying sober. Likewise, to know that as a man I am sexually vulnerable encourages me to take the next two steps.

2. Accept responsibility. Regardless of his age, your man needs to accept responsibility for his sexual behavior. You also need to accept responsibility for your role in his life. Be aware of his changing needs.

Mothers, don't be naive and don't be afraid. Be informed and up-to-date. Let him know you're willing to talk privately, confidentially, and compassionately.

Daughters, fathers go through their own changes, and they are not all easy. If you see him struggling with changes, be ready to help. You also need to be aware of his possible physical concerns. Encourage him to have regular checkups. Be there for him to talk to. Be understanding and nonjudgmental.

Wives, read and talk; talk and read. Stay in touch with the wealth of information from a Christian perspective that is available concerning a healthy sex life. There is some old counsel that I hope you will not think too earthy: "If he is happy with his sex life at home, he will stay at home." Realize that this is not a sure thing, but it does increase your chances, and it will also benefit your relationship.

Too many Christians are still uncomfortable with clear and honest discussions regarding their sexual relationships. Isn't it sad that we're unable to talk about something which God gave us to enjoy? Nobody would blush if we talked about praying together. Neither would they blush if we talked about loving others. But if we talk about sexual relations between husband and wife, that somehow becomes inappropriate conversation for Christians. So we stuff our fears and feelings, and we pile on the shame.

Don't be angry and offended if you catch your man looking at someone else. You can ignore it or acknowledge it, but keep your sense of humor. My wife will often say, "Cute, huh?"

> *Don't be angry and offended if you catch your man looking at someone else. You can ignore it or acknowledge it, but keep your sense of humor.*

I'll usually come back with something like "Yes, but the difference is that I *love* you."

I appreciate Ingrid's attitude. If you're offended or troubled, then talk about it. If you need more assurance from him, tell him so. Help your man be responsible.

3. Seek accountability. Mr. Rights need to seek accountability. We have already talked about how you can be a positive part of their life. Now encourage them to develop deep, open, and committed friendships with other men. I belong to a group of four men who meet together on a planned regular basis. We have grown to the point where we can put just about anything on the table, and not only is there not any shock or condemnation, but also there is almost always immediate recognition and empathy. After all, we are all men. Additionally, one of those men, my coauthor, is one with whom I have spent hours and hours talking about all manner of things that I would not share openly.

Your man needs intimate relationships with other men, relationships in which accountability grows with trust and familiarity. Let him know that such openness and responsibility make him more attractive in your eyes. Tell him you think it's masculine and sexy. He'll go.

Yes, sexual attraction is a big temptation to most men. Understand and accept that, and help him feel good about it through admitted vulnerability, accepted responsibility, and sought-after accountability.

> *Remember that men do not share their feelings easily, and to admit to feeling inadequate is a definite masculine no-no.*

Self-doubt. You may be thinking that this is not an area of temptation or concern for your Mr. Right, but don't start skipping pages yet. It's not a good practice to generalize, so let me say that most men will have feelings of self-doubt and inadequacy from time to time. These feelings may be more accentuated during some phases of his life. At other times they may not be as obvious. Remember that men do not share their feelings easily, and to admit to feeling inadequate is a definite masculine no-no.

Being a competitive and comparative species, men are always asking themselves, "How do I measure up? Am I good enough? Am I OK?" This will be true in sports, in his career, as a husband and father, as a lover, and too often, as a Christian. In this last area, if he has a good understanding of the gospel, he will recognize that he is not good enough but that he does have a Substitute "who is able to keep you from falling and to present you before his glorious presence without fault and with great joy" (Jude 24).

In addition, he needs you as wife, mom, daughter, sister, or friend to convey acceptance and affirmation. Compliment his strong points. Let him know that you accept him and love him just the way he is. Tell him again and again the things you like about him. He already knows his weaknesses, and he knows that you know them too.

Show him that you look beyond them and see his strengths. After a while you'll be able to talk about some of the deeper issues of his life. He'll even be willing to bring up his own shortcomings because he is now secure in your love.

Aging also creates self-doubt. Many of the things your men relied on to affirm their masculinity in the past can become a source of self-doubt with the passage of time. The simple answer, of course, is to replace those measurements with others, and most men do, but the changeover is still not easy, and it leaves them in doubt. A boy transfers from elementary to middle school with uncertainty and doubt. There are new rooms, new kids, new rules, and new expectations. You smile, but do you remember as well? I do. Then just when he gets settled in, he's off to high school with those big kids. Will he be accepted? Will he make the team? When a young man makes the transition to college, he truly encounters another world. The values can be very different. Some of the most popular jocks in high school wash out in college, because the old identity was good only in high school, and they can't seem to find a new one.

The next transition is into the workplace. Another beginning, another challenge, and another opportunity for self-doubt. It's also another time of having to prove himself with new rules and objectives. Most men do fairly well through all these steps. But they encounter more self-doubt than they are willing to admit. You need to be aware of

Aging also creates self-doubt. Many of the things your men relied on to affirm their masculinity in the past can become a source of self-doubt with the passage of time.

that. If you have a man in your life going through one of these transition periods, find ways to affirm him other than by his performance. His gifts, talents, and abilities may not be those you had hoped he would possess. But encourage his interests, and assure him of your unconditional love and support.

The more difficult transitions usually come during midlife, which usually appears sometime between 35 and 55. By now physical performance is showing some signs of deteriorating. While this is usually an acceptable and often humorous subject, it can be more traumatic for some men than others. I don't think any of us enjoy midlife transition, but most men manage. Some men begin to evaluate themselves on a broader scale: "Where am I in my career?" "What are my current goals?" "What are my realistic options?" Some men still have a lot of choices available and will continue to expand their productivity. Many will realize that they aren't going to climb any further and that they're never going to reach the goals they set for themselves 20 years earlier. They begin to feel that the best years are behind them and that they weren't good enough. Now what do they do? They can realistically lower their sights, but that's demoralizing. They can change course, which obviously has its dangers. Or they can deny reality, buy a sports car, wear a gold chain, maybe get an ear pierced, and act like a younger man again. The latter choice works for some for a while, but it doesn't fool anybody, and it doesn't last.

Glitches in making transitions are normal. Don't be alarmed or frightened. Offer encouragement and understanding.

What can you do? Once again, be there and be aware. Glitches in making transitions are normal. Don't be alarmed or frightened. Offer encouragement and understanding. Don't laugh unless you are truly laughing with him and not at him. Encourage communication. Acquaint him with an older mentor who has already successfully been through a midlife transition.

I see a new transition on the horizon that may be much more difficult than midlife crisis. We have a whole generation of young men who are going to face personal evaluation at a much earlier age. The baby busters are hitting the workplace and finding many of the desirable jobs they were preparing for already taken because of the large numbers of baby boomers still in the work force. The younger men are well educated, but there is no place to go. They have the same lofty dreams, but reality keeps popping their balloons. They are the first modern generation that cannot expect to have a higher standard of living than their parents. It's like having a midlife crisis at 25. These men are going to need a lot of help and support.

Two other major transitions can shake a man's self-confidence. One is retirement. Many men long for the day when they can set aside the daily grind and just do as they please. Sounds great, and for some it is, but for many more it's a nightmare. If a man's identity has been wrapped up in what he did, it's going to be difficult for him to retire. A man needs to feel needed. He needs to feel like he contributes something. Husbands and wives have frequently adjusted through the years to not spending much time together. Now they are together all the time. If the finances are tight, this can be a very depressing transition. Encourage involvement. If travel is not an option or an interest, then help your man find clubs and organizations that truly need him. Encourage friendships with other retired men. Remind him of the good work he has done, but assure him that you love him for who he is today, not for what he did yesterday.

> **If a man's identity has been wrapped up in what he did, t's going to be difficult for him to retire. A man needs to feel needed.**

The final difficult step comes when a man is no longer able to care for himself. This is hard for both sexes, but men often resist more. Losing his driver's license is almost worse than taking away an arm or a leg. Becoming a dependent again is not a pleasant change, and he needs closeness and assurance more than ever. This can be the hardest time for you, his supporter. Try to guard his dignity and pride. Ask for help. Find the agencies and volunteers who are trained to assist you in this last and least dignified transition.

Time. Many, if not most, men are tempted to spend more time on the things that affirm their own masculinity now and less time on the people who really matter. That's going to be challenging to change, yet I would encourage you not just to accept it either. One approach may be for you to initiate sincere interest in his work, outside hobbies, or recreational activities. Ask questions and listen attentively. Become knowledgeable about his work. This is particularly valid in the husband/wife relationship, but the same principle applies for any woman wanting to strengthen her relationship with any of the men in her life.

Certainly one of if not the biggest time wasters and relationship killers is the television. It is fine if you have a few favorite programs that you enjoy watching together. Otherwise shut it off and do something together. Balance is the key. Your man may enjoy watching sports, but you may prefer a documentary or a movie. Work out a plan together without nagging or neglect. Talk about and make a list of things you actually enjoy doing together. This may take a little initiative and work to begin with, but the rewards are worth it. Showing some genuine enthusiasm for some of his choices will often help him go along with some of yours.

Your man may struggle with a host of personalized temptations, but hang in there. Love him, and resist a few of your own enticements. Resist the temptation to

❤ sell him. (The market isn't too good right now.)

❤ trade him. (His replacement will still be male.)

❤ change him. (It doesn't work.)

❤ leave him. (He can't send you alimony because he doesn't know where the bank is, and you know he won't ask for directions.)

❤ give up. (You don't really want him to stay that way, do you?)

❤ send him back to his mother. (Why do you think she moved when you got married?)

❤ stop loving him. (He needs you.)

CHAPTER 9

►◄

Is Sex Really Necessary?

S ex is like fire. In a fireplace it's warm and delightful, but outside the hearth, it's destructive and uncontrollable. The apostle Paul put it more succinctly: "But if they cannot control themselves, they should marry, for it is better to marry than to burn with passion" (1 Cor. 7:9). Sex is not the only reason to marry, of course, but marriage is the fireplace in which God designed the flames of passion to be fanned. Nothing can ruin the fireplace of marriage faster than failure to understand the fuel it contains—sex.

Men want sex, and women want relationships. Men want flesh, and women want love. Men can respond just about anytime, but women are more cyclical. Men turn on quickly, whereas women often take more time. For men, sex is a high priority, but for women it's one of many priorities. This tremendous difference in sexual fuel is not something we can do a great deal about. It's just the way God designed us.

High concentrations of testosterone acting on a male brain and mediated through the hypothalamus mean that boys are much more sexually active (on the average) than girls. They have nocturnal emissions, they seek sexual gratification with a greater appetite, and although they mature at a later age, they tend to have sexual intercourse at an earlier age.

The average man knows, often all too well, what his genitalia look like. He sees them daily. He also knows what other men's genitalia look like and how he measures up. The average woman, until very recent times, had no idea what her genitalia looked like; many still don't. Many women are unaware that the vagina, the labia majora and minora, the vaginal wall and its excretory gland, are as complicated and interesting a set of genital organs as the man's.

Another cause of misunderstanding between sexes is that a woman may go into adult life without ever experiencing an orgasm.

PUWMR-5

A normal man cannot. The basic difference in male/female physiology is crucial. A man's orgasm, unlike a woman's, serves a secondary and crucial function of releasing the tension of retained semen and sperm. After puberty a male constantly manufactures semen and sperm. This is dammed up and eventually creates pressure that is both painful and sexually stimulating. To release the accumulated fluid, a spontaneous nocturnal emission, accompanied by an orgasm, will be physiologically induced. Since it is often accompanied by an erotic dream, this is euphemistically called a "wet dream."

Either through nocturnal emission or masturbation, a man understands orgasm and what is required to attain one. On the other hand, a woman is often confused and unsure whether or not she has experienced orgasm. Some cultures, through removal or mutilation of the clitoris, have tried to destroy all sexual pleasure for a woman. Other cultures have attempted to remove the potential for female orgasm through psychological mutilation or religious laws. Until recent years it wasn't well known that God had designed women to experience sexual stimulation and enjoyment just as men do. The clitoris is actually God's gift to women so that they can enjoy the sex act as much as a man. It should be noted that this gift of female sexual enjoyment was reserved for humankind and not given to the animal kingdom.

It should be noted that this gift of female sexual enjoyment was reserved for humankind and not given to the animal kingdom.

Even though God designed women to enjoy sex as much as men, this act doesn't often hold priority in the female psyche. Men deprived of sex are much more likely to become morose and irritable. Women rarely experience the same feeling of deprivation in a celibate state. What they miss is the companionship of sex. Men just miss sex.

• • •

To a far greater extent than is often acknowledged, men are penis-oriented. In many respects the penis is the center of a man's identity. It is the axis around which the male body and personality rotate. That the penis is central to a man's identity is also indicated by the number of nicknames that have been assigned to it. Do we have nicknames for arms and legs and livers? Not even buttocks and breasts come close to the number of terms that have been given to the penis. One author listed more than 50 general terms used to identify it.

The point is that in a man's psyche the penis is king. Unfortunately, it sometimes acts in an unpredictable fashion. The reason the penis sometimes seems to have a mind of its own and to act contrary to its master's wishes is that a man is not always in touch with what he really thinks and feels. The male organ thus becomes an instrument of public record that announces his innermost thoughts, cravings, and fantasies.

Your Mr. Right cannot fool his penis. It has a direct line to his brain. If he's angry, nervous, or worried and tries to hide his feelings by putting on a happy, sexy exterior, his penis will know the truth. If he's feeling sexually attracted but suppressing it for social reasons, his penis will know the truth. If you offend or hurt your husband, no matter how much he tries to conceal his feelings his penis will act hurt or offended. If you adore your partner, flatter him, and desire him sexually, his penis will respond accordingly, even if he doesn't think he's in the mood.

In a sense the behavior of your man's penis is a more accurate barometer of who he is at any particular moment than his own conscious assessment. A woman can perform sexually whether interested or not. She can lovingly oblige her mate even if she is not in the mood. A man cannot, by the peculiar nature of his genitalia, do what is not exciting to do. If he has no desire or is frightened for any number of reasons, he will fail. Just as his sexual appetite is advertised, so also his impotence is publicly announced.

Since the penis is still not a topic for polite conversation in many Christian circles, you may be interested to know the bottom-line meaning of this interesting appendage—*power*. For the most part, men behave in the bedroom much the same way they behave in the living room, office, factory, freeway, or whatever. Throughout history phallic symbols have been used to indicate power. In our modern society these symbols come in many forms. The most widely viewed phallic symbol today is a man's automobile. What is there about the automobile that makes it the ultimate phallic symbol of our male culture?

> *A woman can perform sexually whether interested or not. A man cannot, by the peculiar nature of his genitalia, do what is not exciting to do. If he has no desire or is frightened for any number of reasons, he will fail.*

Primarily, it's a machine, and historically, machines have been used to enhance male power and force. Levers, pulleys, gears, and wheels were invented to increase men's power. Now all these power symbols are represented in a single machine, the automobile, which signifies power, status, speed, armor, and sex.

Why do we limit our highway speed to 65 miles an hour but build automobiles that are capable of 150 miles an hour? Why do we produce vehicles that will go from zero to 60 in less than four seconds? There's no real reason for the creation of powerful cars except for the psychological purpose they serve. Sitting behind the wheel of a red Corvette helps a man disguise his sense of inadequacy.

In fact, when a man is seated in the driver's seat, his behavior often changes dramatically. Protected by steel armor, capable of flight if things turn against him, the average man can be reduced to a competitive, aggressive idiot. Life-threatening behavior is a commonplace event on our highways. If someone cuts a man off, endangering his life while traveling more than 60 miles an hour, the logical (an often vaunted male attribute) action would be for the man to keep his distance from the offender. But a man rarely responds that way. He interprets this aggression as humiliation, as a personal assault, or perhaps as a challenge to his manhood that must be met. If his life was endangered, he'll get even by racing ahead and cutting the other fellow off, thus endangering his life a second time. Logical? No. Masculine? Yes.

The loving attention a man pays to his car is difficult for many women to understand. After all, it is only transportation. Wrong! When a man polishes his automobile, he is really polishing his own self-image—in particular his sexual image. The expensive automobile is actually a form of male jewelry.

The way to a man's heart may be through his stomach, but the way to his identity is through his penis. If you want to make your relationship something that novels are written about, make your man's sexual satisfaction a high priority. Make him happy, and he'll make you happy. Give to him, and you're more likely to get what you want from him.

• • •

If your Mr. Right does not let you know what he likes sexually, you can do one of three things: (1) forget about it, (2) experiment, or (3) ask. The first alternative is not recommended. Learning what turns him on is very important for a healthy marital relationship. You can experiment, trying different things to see what works. At the very least, this will add excitement to your sex life. But the best way is to ask. Let him know you want to satisfy him.

Some men, especially some Christian males, are uncomfortable with sex talk. If that's the case, be patient. Start slowly by

A woman has tremendous power over a man. She is capable of making him virile or impotent almost at will.

asking his opinion on a book or magazine article dealing with sex. Ask him whether or not he thinks the author is on the right track. You can also ask during lovemaking, "Do you like this?" or "Would you like me to . . . ?" Naturally you want to make sure he understands your likes and dislikes, because his ability to please you will have a direct effect on his self-esteem.

Men have extremely fragile egos, particularly when it pertains to their penises. If you want Mr. Right to improve his lovemaking abilities, use positive reinforcement rather than negative criticism. Try to avoid saying anything that could be taken as a put-down, especially while making love. If you want to correct him or change his behavior, do it with delicacy and compassion. Be honest, but focus on what you'd *like* him to do, not what he's doing wrong. In other words, instead of saying "I can't stand it when you touch me like that," say "I think I'd really like it if you would touch me like this . . ." One form of expression suggests that he's inadequate, whereas the other says he's OK, you love him, and you want everything between you to be even better. A woman has tremendous power over a man. She is capable of making him virile or impotent almost at will.

When your man does something you like, give him immediate positive reinforcement. Let him know you like it. Let him know it makes you feel great. Most men enjoy groans of appreciation even if you feel self-conscious about the words. The slightest sign of pleasure from his woman makes any man feel 10 feet tall. If this sounds childish to you, remember that a man with an erection is more like a child than an adult.

A knowledgeable woman does not have to be told not to call her husband's penis a "cute little thing." No man wants his genitalia referred to as *cute* and certainly not as *little*. It is to be seen as powerful and treated as awesome. How you describe your husband's penis becomes a description of him. You're speaking about his self-esteem, not just his genitalia.

Something to remember: If you want something special from your husband, the absolute worst time to ask is when he is frustrated sexually. Wait until he is sexually aroused and his blood, along with his willpower, has rushed to his loins, and chances are he will grant almost anything you might request. Is this manipulation? Yes. And women in the know have been using it for centuries. However, frequency of use doesn't make such manipulation acceptable.

The biblical rules for sexual harmony are explicit. "The wife's body does not belong to her alone but also to her husband. In the same way, the husband's body does not belong to him alone but also to his wife. Do not deprive each other except by mutual consent and for a time, so that you may devote yourselves to prayer" (1 Cor. 7:4, 5).

The downside to this penis fascination of males is that sex often becomes a command performance rather than a fun-filled happening. Sex was designed by God to be life's most inexpensive luxury in a marriage relationship. But for too many men it has become a worrisome task, a source of tension, or a burden rather than an escape mechanism from the stresses of life.

> *Most men find a sexually aggressive woman a great turn-on. They love it when a woman initiates sex. They love being seduced.*

Sex is good for your Mr. Right's mood and his outlook on life. It's a natural tranquilizer, with no bad side effects. Men who are frustrated sexually tend to be tense and irritable; they often seem angry at the world. However, men who are sexually satisfied tend to feel good about themselves and to have a positive outlook on life. Also, as a purely physical exercise, sex is highly recommended. It is excellent for cardiovascular fitness; it benefits circulation; it stimulates the nervous system and the prostate gland; it clears up mental cobwebs; it invigorates the whole body.

Common Female Complaints

He wants to have sex when I'm not in the mood. Typically men want sex more often than do women, and many men expect their partner to deliver on demand. Assuming the relationship is working on all other levels, a smart woman will do everything she can short of jeopardizing her health to enable her man to feel good about himself. Sex is one of those opportunities.

Naturally, at times sex is not appropriate, and you will say no. Only the most self-centered man wouldn't understand that. By the same token, there are times when it's appropriate to say yes even if you'd rather be doing something else. Every couple have to work out their own ground rules. But in general a woman who wants a happy, healthy man will try to be there for him whenever (and wherever) he wants her.

What if he turns me down when I want him? Most men find a sexually aggressive woman a great turn-on. They love it when a woman initiates sex. They love being seduced. But it's also true that men can be threatened by an *overly* aggressive woman. Ordering your man to have an erection is not the same as seducing him.

Admittedly, some men do not appreciate it when a woman initiates sex. The more conservative the male, the more likely he is to view initiating sex as his exclusive territory. Others simply interpret a woman's assertiveness as demanding and are turned off sexually.

If your man does not respond, perhaps the timing is wrong or he's too busy at the moment. If so, make an appointment. Tell him you want to set aside a definite time to devote entirely to lovemaking. Rent a motel room near his office or place of work if you have to. It will do wonders to rekindle the romance flame in your fireplace.

He's doesn't want to have any fun with sex. It's strictly "taking care of business." Many men get overly serious when having sex because they're

> **Sex should provide mutual pleasure, not pain. You absolutely must let him know he's hurting you. Tell him gently; don't whine or get angry, so that he doesn't take it as negative criticism or a sign of failure.**

concerned about their performance. They're afraid that if they relax and have fun, they'll lose their desire or their erection. For some men a loss of erection is the ultimate humiliation. Assure him that you know how to resurrect his erection if he should happen to lose it.

Or you may have to accept the fact that your man will be all business once he is turned on. Sex is the ultimate in goal-oriented male behavior. Some of your man's traits you can change; others you need to accept or accommodate to.

Sometimes he's too rough, and it hurts. Sex should provide mutual pleasure, not pain. Often a man is too clumsy or rough during foreplay. Since he often desires you to put a "death grip" on his penis, he may assume you enjoy the same amount of pressure. You absolutely must let him know he's hurting you. Tell him gently; don't whine or get angry, so that he doesn't take it as negative criticism or a sign of failure.

Sometimes pain occurs during sexual intercourse. This could result from too much internal friction, which might be solved by a vaginal lubricant. Sometimes thrusting too hard against the pubic bone or the twisting of your body in an awkward manner is painful. In such cases, you have a responsibility to help him change his habits so that you both can enjoy the experience.

He wants to do things I find distasteful. Assuming that he's not trying to force you to do something dangerous or painful, you might want to ask yourself why you find a particular act distasteful. Examine the source of your resistance. Is something inherently dangerous, dirty, or evil about this act? Does the Bible specifically refer to this act as sin? Or do you find it distasteful because you've been brought up to think of it in that manner? These are all personal questions that you must answer for yourself, but I would strongly recommend that you talk it over with your husband. He deserves to know why you find the act distasteful, and you need to understand why he does not.

My husband is always so rushed, and he uses only the missionary position. Our sex life is boring. Educate him. In a gentle way let him know that you enjoy being intimate with him so much that you'd like to savor the experience by slowing down, perhaps lying side by side and taking your time. Later tell him how much you'd like to take the top position the next time you have sex. You might want to get a good Christian sex manual and begin reading it together.

My husband thinks the best way to make up is with sex, but I'm so mad at him that it turns me off. It may take a little time, but try to get over it. If there's a deep rift in your relationship, work it out. If you need a marriage counselor, pick up the phone and make an appointment. But if you're talking about the normal irritations that occur in any relationship, don't let them get in the way of sex. You will both be frustrated and perhaps neglect one of the best solutions to the tension between you.

I'd like to have sex, but my husband is impotent. Whatever its source, impotence or the threat of impotence will haunt many men throughout their lives. The importance of this threat is suggested by the symbolic meaning of the word for sexual failure. *Potency* liter-

> **Whatever its source, impotence or the threat of impotence will haunt many men throughout their lives.**

ally means power. To be impotent is to be disempowered, and to the man, for whom power is almost everything, to be impotent is tantamount to being a nonperson. *Impotent* is a term reserved exclusively for men. That's why many modern sexologists now refer to this condition as being *sexually dysfunctional.*

The first thing your husband should be encouraged to do is to see a urologist. Most impotency can be cured in a relatively short time. Much of it is psychological, but a thorough physical examination should always precede sexual counseling or therapy.

Someone once commented: "If women spent as much time attending to their husband's sexual needs as they devote to their hair, makeup, and clothing, they would get more of what they want and have a much more satisfying relationship with their man." This does not mean that you should become a sex slave to your husband. It does not make you less of a feminist or less than equal to your husband. It does not require you to sacrifice your self-respect. It simply means learning to understand and to accommodate your husband's needs. Approach that task with all the energy and skill you'd bring to any other endeavor, and you'll both be much happier.

Sex Is Temperamental!

Everyone knows that men and women are different physically, but they are also different mentally and emotionally. Their appetites as well as their inhibitions are different. Added to this rich mix of possibilities are inherited temperament traits. Many writers and sex therapists fail to consider the influence of temperament on a couple's love life.

It is inaccurate to assume that women are less aggressive than men. While this may be true when considering an entire population study, it certainly is not true when considering an individual marriage relationship. For example, sanguine women are often more aggressive than phlegmatic men—and they are usually attracted to each other for that very reason.

Sexual expression is more than a physical experience. It involves the mind, emotions, body, mental attitude, temperament tendencies, physical fitness, sex education, and a host of other factors. Just because two people share the same temperament doesn't mean that they are identical or even that much alike. They will, however, share some common characteristics that make it relatively easy to identify their temperament blend. Tim LaHaye in his book *Your Temperament: Discover Its Potential* offers some interesting temperament snapshots to help you understand Mr. Right's inherited sexual tendencies.

> *Sexual expression is more than a physical experience. It involves the mind, emotions, body, mental attitude, temperament tendencies, physical fitness, sex education, and a host of other factors.*

Sammy Seller—He is so responsive that it takes very little to turn him on. Since he is so obvious about everything he does and feels, it should be easy for you to be instantly aware of his mood. He usually has a tremendous appetite for everything, including sex.

Sammy Seller generally has very few hang-ups about sex and

usually makes it quite clear that he enjoys it. Sex usually ranks number one or two on his list of favorite things to do. Sammy is often reluctant to take no for an answer. In fact, you can easily hurt his feelings or deflate his ego by not responding with a positive gesture.

Underneath he has a great need for affection and affirmation. If these needs are not met at home, he'll often seek them elsewhere. Of all the temperament types, Sammy Seller is the most easily tempted sexually. Because he is weak-willed, emotionally excitable, and needs to feel appreciated, he is very vulnerable to an unscrupulous woman.

A sanguine generally has very few hang-ups about sex and usually makes it quite clear that he enjoys it.

Sammy can be very romantic and easily instructed in the art of bringing his wife to orgasm. You may have to repeat the instructions from time to time, since a sanguine has a short attention span and often lacks self-control.

Sally Seller—She is cheerful, happy, affectionate, and has the ability to make men feel comfortable in her presence. Her charming personality makes her an instant target for any male's "hit" parade. She is often surprised when men "come on" to her, since she was only being friendly.

As a wife, she has a tremendous amount of love to impart to her husband and family. Lovemaking is very important to her, and it doesn't take much coaxing to get her in the mood. She rarely has hang-ups about anything, so she usually has a positive attitude toward sex and trying something new. Her natural ability to express herself overcomes her inhibitions, and she heightens her sexual enjoyment by becoming aggressive. Sally Seller starts out in marriage expecting sex to be fun, and she's seldom disappointed, because of her positive attitude. She can endure almost anything in a marriage as long as she is not starved for love.

Donald Doer—On the surface he seems to be sensitive and caring during the courtship days. However, once married, he seems to focus his energy on new challenges. For Donald Doer the difference between courtship and marriage is often the difference between the pictures in the seed catalogue and what actually comes up in the garden.

Doer is goal-oriented! During your courtship his goal was to attain you. Having attained that goal, he probably has established other, more pressing goals in his life. However, when he's in the mood for sex, you once again become an immediate short-term goal. His attitude may leave you feeling frustrated or used, even if the sex is good.

When confronted with your complaint that he doesn't love you anymore, he often responds, "Of course I love you; don't I work and slave to provide for you and the kids?" Emotionally he is an extremist—either hot or cold. He can get furiously angry over nothing and then want sex an hour or so later. Showing affection is difficult for Doer unless it helps him attain a goal.

Even though he may not have received any real sex education, he will often refuse to admit that he needs help in the love-making department. But since he's always practical, he can be taught by a patient and

For a choleric male the difference between courtship and marriage is often the difference between the pictures in the seed catalogue and what actually comes up in the garden.

loving wife. He learns quickly and may even begin to identify your emotions and moods without being prompted.

Doris Doer—Usually an exciting creature, she's extremely active in every area of life. Forceful, dynamic, and goal-oriented describe her fast-paced lifestyle. She often has a sarcastic personality combined with a razor-blade tongue that dominates and controls everyone in her presence.

She can be an excellent sexual partner if she has been raised with a positive attitude toward sex. However, if she has been taught that sex is dirty, the opinionated Doer finds it extremely difficult to change her mind. But once convinced that God wants her to enjoy sex, she's a quick study and can make a rapid transition.

Her aggressive attitude may be so intimidating to her husband that their sex life may suffer. It is important for Doris Doer to learn how to affirm her husband in order to establish a consistent and satisfying sex life. To her credit, she will usually adjust and become a very enjoyable sex partner once she learns how important sex is to her husband and how the fragile male ego is attached directly to his penis.

> *More than any other temperament, the melancholy has the capacity to express true love. When his sex life is good, he will overextend himself in other areas of the marriage in thoughtfulness, kindness, and emotion.*

Her greatest task will be to avoid heaping criticism, sarcasm, and ridicule upon her husband, particularly as it pertains to sex. Doris Doer exudes so much self-confidence that her mere presence may be enough to make her husband impotent at times.

Tommy Thinker—A superidealist, he often goes into marriage without any sex education, because he believes it will just all work out. If he's blessed with an amorous and exciting wife who has no hang-ups, everything usually does work out. But if he marries someone as naive as he, they may have difficulty adjusting to each other's sexual needs and desires.

More than any other temperament, Tommy Thinker has the capacity to express true love. He is usually a loyal and faithful partner. When his sex life is good, he will overextend himself in other areas of the marriage in thoughtfulness, kindness, and emotion.

Among his greatest assets are his romantic inclinations and creativity. He prepares thoroughly with soft music, dim lights, and other things that delight the romantic heart of a woman. Because he's very analytical, he quickly learns what his wife finds pleasurable and enjoys bringing her fulfillment.

However, his perfectionist tendencies can also be his ruination. I read about one Thinker husband who became extremely turned on as he watched his wife undress, but then lost his erection when she didn't hang up her clothes.

If his wife does not respond immediately to his suggestion of sex, he will interpret her actions as total rejection. If his wife happens to be in a coy mood and wants a little coaxing, she will not usually find it with her Thinker mate. However, Tommy Thinker has a tremendous amount of love to give when given the slightest encouragement.

Teresa Thinker—She's an unpredictable partner because of her tremendous mood swings. On some occasions she'll be as dynamic as Doer or as stimulating as Seller. At other times she has absolutely no interest in anything—including sex.

The supreme romantic, when in the mood for sex she prepares for it carefully with dinner by candlelight, soft music, heavy perfume, and a revealing negligee. Although she's capable of enjoying ecstatic love

The kindest of all temperaments, the phlegmatic rarely embarrasses or insults his wife, because sarcasm is just not his way.

at heights that would asphyxiate other mortals, she rarely is interested in setting world records for frequency. Her motto is that quality is *always* superior to quantity.

She may exhibit a prudishness that inhibits her sexual enjoyment, especially if her mother had a problem with sexual hang-ups. She may misuse religious arguments to excuse her sexual abstinence, but her real problem is a misunderstanding of God's gift of sexuality. She may be the type who saves sex only for propagation—rarely for pleasure.

Of all temperaments, she's the most likely to use sex as a weapon, or at least as a reward for what she considers appropriate behavior. What she doesn't realize is that she is cheating herself out of both the enjoyment of sex as well as the loving approval of her husband.

Robert Relater—Some assume that because a phlegmatic is easy-going and may lack motivation, he may not be a very energetic lover, but that may not always be true. He usually accomplishes more than he is given credit for, especially in the lovemaking arena. He doesn't brag a lot about his sexual skills, but they're usually sufficient.

The kindest of all temperaments, Robert Relater rarely embarrasses or insults his wife, because sarcasm is just not his way. He rarely gets angry and seldom creates irritation in others. He is the master of the "soft answer."

Believing that good things come to those who wait, he is patience personified, apparently able to outwait others into action. His love life is probably like that as he waits for his mate to initiate sex on a fairly frequent basis. A creature of habit, he'll find whatever sexual frequency his mate desires comfortable for him as well.

If things go poorly, he'll likely crawl into a shell of silence, since he usually finds it difficult to talk about anything, especially sex. Consequently he may silently endure an unsatisfying relationship for years and cheat both himself and his partner out of countless ecstatic experiences that God meant for them to enjoy.

Rebecca Relater—Usually the easiest person in the world to get along with, she loves to please people and usually gives in to her more forceful mate rather than create a turmoil. She is easily satisfied and often turns her affection on her children if there's trouble between her and her husband.

Her passive personality means that she rarely initiates sex, but because she wants to please him, she almost never turns him down. Fear tends to be a dominating force in her life, and she is often afraid of displeasing her husband.

She may become careless about her appearance and may need a gentle reminder that her husband is aroused through the eye-gate. If she ceases to care how she looks, not only will she lose her self-esteem, but her husband's love and respect will also fade if this condition is not corrected.

She requires a strong, gentle husband who understands a woman's body and takes time to arouse her to orgasm. Once she has learned the art of orgasm, her desire for that experience will help overpower her tendency to passivity, and she can learn to be an exciting partner. Since words do not come easy to Rebecca Relater, she'll need an expressive husband who talks to her about sex without embarrassment.

• • •

One of the advantages of understanding the four temperaments is that it becomes easier to appreciate why Mr. Right acts or reacts the way he does. That in turn helps you accept his individual foibles and work with them, not against them.

By understanding your Mr. Right, you can learn to cooperate rather than clash, to affirm rather than criticize, and in the process you will develop a long and enjoyable sexual relationship. One of my favorite authors reminds us: "Those who marry enter a school from which they are never in this life to be graduated" (Ellen G. White, *The Adventist Home,* p. 105).

CHAPTER 10

What Your Man Is Afraid to Ask About His Fears

O ne of the most valuable skills you can acquire as a woman is to be able to help your Mr. Right deal with his fears. The trick, of course, is to do it without letting on that you know about them. Our society teaches that men are not supposed to be afraid. I (Marvin) know that a lot of recent information attempts to strip away that supposition, but I'm afraid the bottom line is that men still want and need to be perceived as fearless. We want to be strong. We want to be tough. We want to be brave. To admit that we need help seems to be counterproductive to our self-image. However, it is possible for you to help your men without their knowing that they are being helped.

In an ideal situation this help would begin during the early years of life. How neat it would be for a mother, a grandmother, or even an older sister to begin to draw out the uncertainties a boy faces as he begins school, anticipates a stressful doctor's appointment, or grieves through his first loss of a beloved pet! To be able to affirm his masculinity, while at the same time to help him admit his feelings, would be a ministry of great value. Obviously a father, grandfather, or older brother can also accomplish this task if he has completed the prerequisite of going through that process in his own life. The secret is in showing sensitivity.

A sample statement at an appropriate time might be something like this: "I'm so proud of you. I remember how afraid I was in a similar situation." If a boy has role models who are willing to admit their fears and yet face them, he will obviously handle his own fears more successfully.

As a young man enters the girl-watching stage (for some that begins at age 4), he needs a balanced feminine perspective. He desperately wants reassurance at this stage but will seldom ask for it. The adolescent male has a body that plays all kinds of tricks on him. Changes are happening literally overnight, and they're bewildering to say the least. To make matters worse, he is thrown into a junior high gym class and required to strip with a group of other boys all at different stages of development. If he is slower to develop, he may well experience a sense of inadequacy. Conversely, if he is ahead of the average pace, he may display a sense of superiority. One of the most damaging misconceptions we men carry into adulthood is status by comparison. Mothers, in particular, can play an enormous role in containing this damage by providing a solid sense of acceptance. They can teach Mr. Right that self-esteem is not based on comparisons.

Young adult males are leaving home, marrying, and entering their careers much later than previous generations. Their fathers and grandfathers often have a tendency to be critical of this tardiness and seem to be implying, "If you were a man, you'd be out there taking responsibility as I did." What a golden opportunity for an alert woman to help him confront some of his doubts! Don't approach these doubts as fears, for even the modern male is reluctant to admit he is afraid. Help your man accept his individual strengths and not feel threatened by comparisons. To be sure, a fellow may need a fire built under his seat, but this needs to be done in a way that leaves him feeling like a man.

> *To be sure, a fellow may need a fire built under his seat, but this needs to be done in a way that leaves him feeling like a man.*

Without question the most critical time in a man's life is during his midlife years. All of a sudden, or so it seems, all the things he has looked to for his assurance of manliness are beginning to show signs of change. Unfortunately, each change is almost never for the better as far as he's concerned. He realizes with great reluctance that his prime is past, his peak is piqued, his libido is laborious, and his courage is crumbling. In a last-ditch effort to deny it all and run from his fears, he grabs every outward opportunity to recapture the appearance of youth. This is usually so obvious that friends, family, and even casual acquaintances just smile, but to the midlife male the laughter is easier to cope with than the fears of reality.

If this describes your spouse, dad, son, brother, or friend, he needs all the understanding, compassion, and affirmation he can get. Pray that he will make it through this difficult transition without doing something he will later regret. Again, an older man can often share some sage advice at this point. However, the midlife male may observe some of the physical challenges facing his older mentor and cling to his second childhood even more tenaciously. While it is true that every man is different—and certainly not all men go through such a noticeable midlife crisis—I believe that some of the changes looming out there make all of

Unfortunately, sexual knowledge has been slow to achieve acceptance in Christian circles. Isn't that sad? Christians ought to have a clear and accurate picture of how God made us. However, we rarely seem to be able to talk about it.

us tremble with fear—at least a little. These impending changes fall into four categories:

1. Sexual concerns—Perhaps the greatest fear a man faces is declining sexual performance (at least in his perception), or impotence. If he has a spouse who is sensitive to his feelings and is willing to lead him gently through this emotional mine field, he's blessed with an angel of God. An old saying states: "The first time you can't perform the second time is a disappointment, but the second time you can't perform the first time is a nightmare." That was funny . . . once. I guess it's an old saying because the problem is not a new one. But there's an abundance of good news for the man who has a knowledgeable and sensitive wife.

Unfortunately, sexual knowledge has been slow to achieve acceptance in Christian circles. Isn't that sad? Christians ought to have a clear and accurate picture of how God made us. However, we rarely seem to be able to talk about it. You wouldn't believe some of the comments we receive while presenting seminars on sexual issues. Talk about phobias!

But let's go on. Let your Mr. Right know that you're endeavoring to understand him. Also let him know that you love and accept him just the way he is. Compliment the physical aspects that you find attractive. Be an informed and sensitive mate.

Men's sexual orientation can certainly cause them to see a situation somewhat differently than a woman. Sometimes you'll be challenged as you attempt to understand your man's thinking process. You may have heard about the famed Moscow Circus, featuring a beautiful woman as the world's premier lion tamer. She demonstrated unbelievable control over the animals, and at the height of the show the fiercest lion of all came meekly up to her, put his paws around her, and nuzzled her with affection.

The crowd went crazy and thundered its approval. A single dissenter was a trucker who declared, "What's so great about that? Anybody can do it."

The ringmaster, somewhat annoyed, challenged him, "Would you like to try it?"

The trucker replied, "I sure would, but first you have to get that lion out of there!"

As pointed out in our previous book, *First-Class Male,* men usually have an obsession with sex. Men also have another obsession related to sex—their fear of talking intelligently about it. Dr. Abraham Morgentaler, who specializes in male infertility and impotency at Beth Israel Hospital, in Boston, and is professor of urological surgery at Harvard Medical School, states: "Men in general have kept themselves very much in the dark regarding their own bodies. This lack of self-knowledge then leads to two kinds of problems: One is that they may not recognize problems or symptoms for which they should seek attention, like getting screened for prostate cancer and performing testicular self-exams. The other is that they may worry that some change in their body is serious when it's not" *(Men's Confidential,* March 1994, p. 9). He often sees men who are assertive and confident in every way except when it comes to talking about their own bodies.

"They come in, and they hem and they haw, and they have difficulty referring to any part by its proper name, and they say, 'I've got a problem down there.' They usually have talked to no one about it; their wives or their partners may know about it, but it has been difficult to actually talk

> *One of the greatest joys to be discovered by mutual understanding and education is that many sexual and physical problems are both common and treatable.*

about. But within a few minutes of being with someone who is nonjudgmental and willing to listen, most men will just open up and feel very relieved. For many men, it's the first time they've been able to talk openly about their bodies" *(ibid.).*

Sexual dysfunction and related fears are difficult for the average man to talk about, but it's much easier with someone who is nonjudgmental and willing to listen. I'm in no way blaming women for this failure to communicate. I am saying that, armed with knowledge and sensitivity, you can create an atmosphere that will do wonders for both of you. Isn't it amazing that we can be married and enjoy a sexual relationship for many years and still find it difficult and embarrassing to talk about it?

One of the greatest joys to be discovered by mutual understanding and education is that many sexual and physical problems are both common and treatable. Men often wince at the thought of erectile dysfunction, whereas women may attribute it to lack of interest. The truth is that erectile dysfunction affects as many as 15 percent of men by age 50 and one out of four by age 60.

Knowing they aren't alone with their problem is encouraging in itself. Understanding that a variety of treatments is available, many of them quite simple, is a gift of life. Read! Talk to each other! Talk to your doctor! Do be careful, however, because your man's ego may be more fragile than your own in the sexual arena.

Many men are trying, at least subconsciously, to live up to a fictional image of what it means to be a man. Men compare what they have and what they do, both materialistically and physically. So handle your man with sensitivity and care. He'll thank you for it in many ways.

Many men fear the word "impotence." You may wish to refer to it as erectile dysfunction. Again, knowledge is power, and it is most powerful when both of you are knowledgeable. Know that erectile dysfunction is common. Almost every man will suffer from erectile dysfunction to some degree at some time in his life. Be prepared for it. Just as having a breast removed can negatively affect a woman's self image, so impotence can negatively impact a man's sexual identity. Some of the major causes include stress and prescription medications. Communication between a husband, wife, and physician can alleviate many of the fears. Treatments vary from simple counseling to a number of medications, topical creams, and therapy involving injections or even implants. You can help by being aware and knowledgeable so that when the problem occurs, you can react affirmingly and sensitively.

> *The gradual enlarging of this gland [prostate] is normal and inevitable. For many men it brings with it a host of nuisances at best and physical problems at worst.*

2. *Physical concerns*—One of the greater physical dangers for a man is the prostate gland. The gradual enlarging of this gland is normal and inevitable. For many men it brings with it a host of nuisances at best and physical problems at worst. Autopsy studies have shown that between 10 and 30 percent of men aged 50 and virtually all men in their 80s have prostate cancer, usually in an early stage and with no symptoms (UC Berkeley *Wellness Letter,* Feb., 1994, p. 6).

A less lethal, but still worrisome problem, involves prostatitis, which results in such symptoms as urgent or frequent urination, pain in the pubic area, post-ejaculatory pain, as well as fever and chills. Prostatitis can be bacterial, in which case it is treated similarly to other infections. Other times it may be nonbacterial and temporary. More serious cases require one of several treatments. If your Mr. Right has problems with urination or prostate pain, urge him to see a urologist. If he is hesitant, contact the American Cancer Society or your local library for articles and pamphlets available to educate both of you.

What do the two of you need to know?

When confined to the prostate gland, prostate cancer is not particularly threatening and is most often curable. The real danger is when it goes undetected and spreads. When that occurs, it becomes life-threatening. Some simple steps can alleviate much of the danger and most of the fear.

Every man more than 40 years old should have an annual DRE (digital rectal exam). This is a painless process, and the discomfort of the apprehension is most often far greater than the reality. The perceived indignity is minuscule compared to the benefits of early detection of any abnormalities. Valuable as the DRE is, it is not enough. Doctors are unable to detect the earliest and, therefore, most treatable tumors. Therefore, he should also have a PSA test, which measures the prostate specific antigen, a protein produced solely by the prostate but circulated throughout the body. An elevated PSA level indicates a potential problem and will detect cancer much earlier than a rectal exam.

Discuss these and other possibilities with your man's urologist, but don't remain ignorant or trust that it will not strike him. There's nothing unmasculine about his being informed about his own body. Make certain he knows how to examine his testicles. If he does not, contact the American Cancer Society or his doctor for more information. This is just as important to your man as the breast self-exam is to you.

Diet also plays an important role in your man's prostate health.

Mounting evidence indicates that a cutback in fat intake, particularly from red meat, would be beneficial not only for his heart but also for his prostate. An article in the October 1993 issue of the *Journal of the National Cancer Institute* indicated a 79 percent higher risk of advanced prostate cancer among men who ate the most fat compared to those who ate the least, and a 164 percent higher risk in those who ate the most red meat compared to those who ate the least. The article pointed out that a dietary change did not necessarily mean a lesser chance of developing prostate cancer, but a lesser chance of its developing into a life-threatening one.

One additional factor in promoting a healthy prostate gland is an active and satisfying sex life. Regular sexual intercourse exercises the prostate and the entire male sexual system, helping keep it functioning properly. Married couples who share an interest in understanding and developing all aspects of their relationship, including this one, will discover it brings valuable rewards far beyond a healthy prostate.

Another looming physical concern for men is heart disease and heart attack. This is still the number one killer, and its contributive factors are legion.

Another looming physical concern for men is heart disease and heart attack. This is still the number one killer, and its contributive factors are legion. Stress, workaholism, denial, macho stereotypes, and a lack of knowledge are typical danger factors for the average man. Early detection is the key. One out of two men dies from complications associated with coronary artery disease. Now, I realize that 100 percent of all men will eventually die from something, but you can help Mr. Right live longer and, more important, even add quality to these additional years.

You may have noticed by now that men are not always eager to know all the facts. This is especially true if it is going to force them to face something they would rather avoid. More often they'll take the attitude that what they don't know can't hurt them.

One old-timer had been in bed for several weeks and simply refused to see a doctor. He didn't need anybody's help. Finally the physicians were called to his bedside despite his angry protests. After they left, the family gathered around to find out what they had said. "Told you I was right. There's nothing to worry about. They just used a lot of big expensive words that nobody understands and finally said, 'Well, there's no use worrying about it. The autopsy will give us the answer soon enough.' "

Thirty minutes of walking at a brisk but comfortable pace at least every other day will make a significant improvement in his health and give him quality time with his significant other (you, providing you walk with him!).

Insist that your Mr. Right have regular checkups. You'll have a lot better chance of sweettalking him into it rather than trying to nag him into it. Unfortunately, many heart disease symptoms don't show up until it's almost too late. Men have a false sense of security because they are able to do their routine chores and to function normally until their arteries are almost completely clogged. While it is true that genetics play a major role, it is also true that prevention plays an even greater part.

Here are a half dozen simple lifestyle changes.

Don't chew the fat! You're probably getting weary of being bombarded with antifat campaigns. The reason you hear so much about it is that fat has such a detrimental affect on health. Fat intake overall is important, but saturated fat intake is critical. Reducing saturated fats will lower LDL cholesterol level as well as blood pressure. These are key factors in reducing a man's risk for heart attack and coronary artery disease. Cut back on his meat intake. He doesn't have to be a vegetarian (although it may be something to consider), but suggest eating meat no more than three times a week. Vegetarians may also be at risk for heart disease. The fats in oils, dressings, sauces, snacks, and the like can be as bad as animal fat. Use olive or canola oils, and even then in limited quantities.

Take a hike! Exercise, exercise, exercise! Exercise will lower blood pressure, reduce cholesterol, burn fat (if he keeps up a good pace for 30 minutes or more), and reduce stress. Thirty minutes of walking at a brisk but comfortable pace at least every other day will make a significant improvement in his health and give him quality time with his significant other (you, providing you walk with him!).

What's up, Doc? That's right. Follow Bugs Bunny's example and crunch a carrot. Carrots have lots of pectin, a cholesterol-lowering fiber. A couple carrots a day could lower his cholesterol as much as 20 percent. Other pectin-rich fruits and vegetables include citrus fruits, tomatoes, potatoes, strawberries, apples, and spinach.

Eat breakfast! Those who skip breakfast tend to have higher cholesterol levels. Fruits, whole-grain breads, and even many ready-to-eat cereals make a better start to the day than fasting. Breakfast skippers often will snack later, and snacks are more likely to be cholesterol-high foods.

The greatest desire most men have in their work is to be respected and admired for the job they do.

Garlic lovers, listen up! Garlic is another way to both lower blood pressure and LDL cholesterol. As little as a clove each day can be helpful, so help yourself. If you're worried about losing a few friends, you can take the odorless capsules, but hey, if you drop dead you're going to lose them anyway, right?

Speak softly and carry a big smile. Anger and internalized stress will raise blood pressure. Studies show that even loud and rapid speech when not angry will send it skyward. Help your Mr. Right relax. Concentrate on slowing his whole body down. Various forms of relaxation, both recreational and meditative, can be beneficial.

Urge him to take time alone, apart from our fast-paced culture.
Women can also benefit from this counsel.

3. Career concerns—The greatest desire most men have in their
work is to be respected and admired for the job they do. A young man
beginning his career will attack obstacles with enthusiasm because he
has been conditioned to be a competitive person. He struggles and
works long hours to make his mark, get noticed, and move up the ladder. About midway through life he begins to deal with reality.

Either he is not going to reach his lofty youthful goals, or he has
reached them and found them to be unsatisfying. He may have sacri-
ficed familial relationships, under the guise of providing for the family, in order to get where he is. What he has left is unrewarding at best.
What's the solution, and how can a woman help? By regular affirma-
tion and assurance that he's respected and admired more for who he is than what he does.

If a man tries to draw closer to God by doing rather than by communicating, accepting, and trusting, he is going to have an insecure relationship.

It is hard to hold back a young man. If you're married to one, you may find that regular communication about what is most important to both of you and daily expres-
sions of love, acceptance, and admiration will help him understand that
he doesn't need to seek those things elsewhere. A man's fear of not
being good enough, of not being acceptable, can cause his competitive
spirit to be blown out of proportion. Fear makes the enemy appear bigger than he actually is.

There's nothing wrong with a man's striving for excellence and
success in the marketplace unless that schedule takes priority over his
other relationships. If you have a close relationship as a wife, mother,
or friend with a young man on his way up, you may have significant
opportunities to help him establish balanced priorities as well as success. Did you know studies have indicated that those husbands who

kiss their wives goodbye in the morning earn more money and achieve higher levels of responsibility than those who do not? What a simple and delightful way to achieve success! The secret is in contentment and being part of a team instead of competing with each other for what is important. I guess that gives new meaning to the term "kissing up."

4. Spiritual concerns—The understanding that men tend to focus on things and activities rather than on relationships may at least partially explain why more women than men attend church. If a man tries to draw closer to God by doing rather than by communicating, accepting, and trusting, he is going to have an insecure relationship. Personally I had a very difficult time grasping God's acceptance of me. I felt I had to do something. I had to be better. This is certainly not exclusive to men, but men do seem predisposed to that kind of thinking.

> *Being informed, as well as being sensitive to the masculine ego, are two very important assets as you attempt to deal with male fears.*

The fear of not being worthy, not being acceptable, leads to comparison, judging, faultfinding, and competition. This interferes with a man's relationship with God as well as with other men. As a result, men may draw away from spiritual thinking and into the world where they have a little more control over what happens.

An active, participatory men's ministry is one of the greatest gifts a church can provide for the men in its community. This is not something that women can do for their men, but it is a ministry they can encourage and support. This ministry doesn't have to be "churchy." In fact, it will be much more successful if it isn't. Men will most easily come together if they have a project to complete, a goal to accomplish, or a game to be played. The church needs to use the natural male pathways in facilitating relationship-building activities.

• • •

In all the areas mentioned in this chapter, the common need is for women to understand that men do have fears, but even many Mr. Rights don't know how to deal with their fears openly or productively. Being informed, as well as being sensitive to the masculine ego, are two very important assets as you attempt to deal with male fears. Time spent working through these fears together will deepen your relationships.

Ingrid and I have worked through several tough times together, and we're closer and more reliant on each other as a result. In fact, the fears we have struggled with the most are now the areas in which we have become the strongest. We have learned to trust God's promise that we "can do everything through him who gives [us] strength" (Phil. 4:13).

Dwelling on a three-way love relationship between you, your Mr. Right, and your God will help dispel most of his fears and phobias. "Fear and love just don't go together. Love dispels fear" (1 John 4:18, Clear Word).